KRISTAL'S WEDDING

Shirley Walston

Dear Reader,

I wrote this book with the intention of giving it to single moms who struggle with too much responsibility and not enough help. It is the true story of my daughter, Kristal, who dreamt of being a mom and a teacher, but died at 16 after a two-year battle with leukemia. It was every mother's nightmare and beyond heartbreaking. Yet we both learned deep lessons about life in the process.

We found hope. Help. We found God—not just some ancient, out-of-date guy who shows up in a hymn on Sundays, but the real, living God. The One who created the earth is the same One who locked His arms around us and stood with us in the midst of suffering. The One who listened to our cries, sent practical help in answer to our prayers. He comforted us, helped us negotiate a car deal and paid off enormous hospital bills. He sustained us when our world threatened to wobble off its orbit.

He exists. He is real. And He wants to help you too! All you have to do is ask.

I'm asking you to help me too. When you finish reading this book, please don't stick it on a shelf somewhere. I want you to find a struggling single mom and give it away. And while she's standing right there, give her a hug for me, will you?

Thanks,
Shirley Walston

CHAPTERS

I
NO HEROICS

"When you stop breathing," the doctor said to my daughter Kristal, "we can try a tracheotomy, which involves making a small incision in your throat to allow...."

"Wait a minute," Kristal said, jerking herself upright. "You're not cutting any holes in MY throat!"

"We can keep a crash cart outside your room to restart your heart..."

"You mean those paddles I've seen them use on TV that make you bounce off the bed? FOR-GIT IT!" she said with fire in her brown eyes. "When I die, I die. You guys are not doing ANY of that stuff to me!"

With his hands at his sides Dr. Kendall listened to my daughter, but didn't say a word. In a typical doctor's scrawl he scribbled "No heroics" on Kristal's hospital chart. Then, clicking his pen, he shoved it into the chest pocket of his wrinkled white coat and shuffled out of the room. The decision was made.

When the doctor had pulled me aside that mid-May morning, asking how far I wanted him to go to save her life, I knew this wasn't a choice I should make solo. Kristal was 16 years old. She was very involved in her own treatment, and we had walked through her leukemia as a duet for almost two years. I knew we had to face this last stanza together.

For weeks, doctors had been saying that the chemo wasn't working anymore. They had even tried experimental drugs to combat her rare form of childhood leukemia, but it had only worked for a few days. Kristal's body was now immune to the drugs that had once wiped out thousands of diseased cells in a day.

This was Kristal's third relapse and her doctors, who had in the beginning given her a 90% chance of survival, no longer offered any hope. The reasons for failure in our nearly two-year battle against cancer were all scientifically reasonable, I supposed. But none of them made it any easier to watch my daughter die.

This was already a stressful time for me. My husband had moved in with another woman. My mother had just died suddenly in the night. As a single parent to Kristal and 6-year-old Jeff, I was also attempting to keep up my All-American dream house on tiny Fox Island and run my own business, a children's clothing store called the Bubblegum Closet in Gig Harbor, an upscale area an hour south of Seattle. I had been hanging on by my un-manicured fingernails for as long as I could remember.

After the doctor left that morning, Kristal and I just held each other. There was nothing much for me to hug anymore. Kristal had always been a solid kid—the kind that thunks like an old Chevy door when you patted her on the back. Now, through her flannel teddy bear pajamas, I could feel every bone. In my never-ending attempt to be brave, I silently wiped away tears.

"When will you be ready to give up?" Kristal asked for the tenth time.

Again I told her, "Not until you breathe your very last breath."

With the medical community abandoning ship, God was our only anchor. What we need at this moment, I thought, is something positive to think about.

"How about planning your wedding?" I suggested hopefully. Someday, I thought—still unwilling to give up on the possibility of a miracle for her even at this stage—we'll need to make these plans. Even if that day never comes, this could be our only chance to discuss such things.

"What time of year will it be?" I began, curling up beside her on the high, white hospital bed.

"Oh, June, I think," she said thoughtfully. "That seems like a good month for a wedding."

"June it is. Which day?"

"How about the sixth? Wasn't that Grandma's birthday?" she asked about my mother, who had died unexpectedly only five weeks earlier.

"Well, her birthday was July 6th, but I'm sure she would appreciate the thought. The sixth sounds good. Where?"

"Let's plan it outside—in a big field, with lots of flowers," she said dreamily, her hands behind her head. I pictured her reclining in that field instead of on a pillow in this sterile hospital room. She couldn't see the bridegroom exactly, she said, but she KNEW he had dark hair and blue eyes. Not an easy combination to find, I noted.

I continued to ask about the maid of honor and bridesmaids. She mentioned Deanna, Kerry, and a few others who had been friends since elementary school. She couldn't decide who would be maid of honor.

Kristal began describing the dresses they would wear. The clothing store owner in me just about gagged when she mentioned the fabric she had in mind—lilac dotted swiss!

"Aauugh!" I croaked. "You've got to be kidding! Have I taught you nothing about fashion? Lilac dotted swiss!?"

"No, no, wait… " she said, shaking her head, the sweet sound of laughter rising from her throat.

"Dotted swiss went out in the '50s! My mother made me a dress of lilac dotted swiss when I was eight!"

"No, no, no," she said, quickly standing her ground. "I swear you'll love this! I saw it in a magazine last week. It's cool. I'll show you. You'll see."

"Okay, okay," I conceded, dismounting from my high horse. "It sounds just awful, but I'm willing to look, but you'll have to convince me. What about your wedding gown?"

Her dress, she said, was made of flowing lace and trimmed with hundreds of pearls. The skirt was gathered from a V at the waist. It had long sleeves, puffy at the top and tight at the forearm, just like most wedding dresses in the 80s. With one of her long, perfect fingernails she traced a V on the back of her hand to show the path the row of seed pearls would take.

As I watched her fall contentedly asleep, the V was still visible on her paper-thin skin. The morning had made me remember Kristal as a little girl. She often spent an hour shoving the furniture around to create an aisle down the green living room carpet, then arranging her stuffed animals and dolls to make sure they could all see over each other's heads.

Then she'd carefully pull on the old white peignoir set someone had given me as a wedding shower gift. When she was finally ready, she'd call me to sing the Dum, Dum, Da Dum, then step-toe-step down the aisle. Skinny blonde pigtails bobbed under the lace and pearl headpiece I'd worn when I married her father. She'd kneel at the coffee table she'd set with grape juice and oyster crackers and marry her perfect groom. From the time she was a preschooler, I just watched and shook my head at her wedding obsession.

Planning Kristal's wedding in the hospital that day was a pleasant, soothing way to spend what began as an awful May morning. I didn't think about it again until weeks later. My mind and emotions were stretched to the limit with Kristal's sickness, the constant care for the house and business and making time to spend with Jeff. It seemed I had to choose on a daily basis who or what would need me most that day.

Until the onset of leukemia, Kristal had a pleasantly boring medical history. It wasn't until my son Jeff, who was nearly 10 years younger than his sister, began the usual toddler falls and regularly needed stitches that we were properly introduced to a hospital emergency ward. Aside from that, even colds were rare at our house.

The change began shortly after Kristal's 15th birthday, with what seemed to me like an attack of laziness. I began to find her napping in the afternoon. She became increasingly pale and listless, which I attributed to her lousy teenage eating habits. She'd been dieting over the summer and gone through jars and jars of dill pickles instead of healthy fruits and vegetables.

A few weeks into her sophomore year, Kristal had a bout with the flu. What she hadn't told me was that she couldn't get up the hill to catch the school bus without sitting down to rest. This former sit-up champ didn't mention that she could now barely do ten in gym class. Still, I thought she was just being lazy and nagged her to stop eating junk food and get involved in after-school activities.

Then a spider bite refused to heal, and she was weaker than ever. Her usually robust skin was pale as buttermilk. In October, I finally insisted she see a doctor.

I arranged for Jeff, who was in kindergarten, to stay later than usual at the babysitter's and somehow shoehorned Kristal's doctor appointment into my schedule. I was confused and surprised when my usually confident and independent 15-year-old clung to me like a kindergartner when the nurse practitioner took a blood sample. She took the vial off for testing and then, within five minutes, returned.

"Please step into the office with me," said the nurse, who had purchased many of her children's clothes from me.

I left Kristal in the exam room and followed.

With her husband/doctor at her side, she matter-of-factly said, "We suspect Kristal has leukemia. I've only seen one case, but that child looked just like Kristal does."

If she said anything about blood tests, I don't recall. Before I had even closed my gaping mouth, she continued on an equally shocking note.

"We've alerted the Oncology unit at Mary Bridge Children's Hospital in Tacoma. They're waiting for you. You need to take her there immediately."

Stunned, I leaned against the doorframe for support. Tears streamed from my eyes, but no words came out of my mouth. My mind screamed, *This can't be! You can't diagnose a disease as serious as leukemia in five minutes! There must be some mistake.*

Determined not to make Kristal panic, I pulled myself together, held my head up and marched back to the examining room to tell Kristal she needed more tests. To protect each other, we pretended not to be scared to death. I went into mother mode—doing what I had to do, smiling as I picked up Jeff and making it sound like an outing as I dropped him at a friend's.

My mind raced through the awful possibilities, but refused to dwell on any of them.

I can only imagine the fear and dread Kristal was feeling. On the drive across the Narrows Bridge to the hospital, our conversation didn't go near our destination, but stuck to small talk. Two doctors and several nurses greeted us at the hospital, obviously waiting for us. They smiled sympathetically and patted our heads with their attitudes.

Why are these people feeling sorry for us? I thought, incensed. *They'll see when they do their dumb tests that nothing's wrong. Just get on with it, I mentally commanded them. Give her some vitamins and get us out of here!*

A young Pediatric Oncologist introduced himself as Dr. Dan. Being in the clothing business, I couldn't help but notice the fashionably faded blue jeans he wore under his white coat. He looked intelligent and competent—until he turned around to reveal a tiny braid that trailed several inches down his back. *Oh brother! What are we doing here?* I thought, scanning the corridor for the white-haired, grandfatherly type doctor that must be behind one of the white doors.

When one didn't materialize, Dr. Dan explained to us the necessity and procedure for the next test, which involved more blood work. This time Kristal calmly offered her arm for more blood to be drawn. Afterward we sat in orange Siamese-twin waiting room chairs, breathing in and glancing around at what would soon become very familiar smells, sights and sounds. Just moments later, the results were in. Dr. Dan asked to see me alone.

"Kristal definitely has leukemia cells in her blood," he said in a small office. "We'll need a bone marrow test to determine the extent of the disease." He went on to explain an awful-sounding procedure that involved driving an eight-inch long needle into her hipbone to draw out the marrow.

Silently nodding, I kept thinking, *This guy's wrong. I know I just returned to church after many long years, but I don't think God would let something this big happen to us right off.*

The doctor asked if I wanted to tell Kristal myself. *Yeah, right! Doesn't every mother long to tell her child she has cancer?* I opted to hold her as he explained about the scary test. As usual, I kept wiping away tears, but Kristal didn't cry. In retrospect, I'm sure she knew that something was very wrong.

We moved into the next room, where everyone seemed to be holding their breaths. Kristal was ordered to lie face down on a table. I held her hand and whispered prayers into her ear as Dr. Dan probed for just the right spot on her anesthetized hip. Once located, he took what looked like a meat thermometer and placed it gently, tip down, on her skin. My prayers intensified. He took the medical version of a ten-inch rubber mallet and expertly struck it with enough force to puncture the bone but not break it.

The next few moments played like a horror movie. I was most aware of Kristal's screams and the vise grip she had on my hand. With the force of a mechanic loosening a heavily rusted eight-inch bolt, the doctor screwed a heavy metal syringe inside the huge needle and suctioned marrow out of the bone. Beads of sweat broke out on his forehead.

Oh, how I wished this was just a bad scene from a movie. Kristal screamed in pain every time he pulled back the plunger to suction off more marrow. He kept at it until he had enough to fill three giant syringes. The black institutional clock on the wall said that the procedure had taken just five minutes, but she and I both swore it felt like days.

We both collapsed with relief when it was over. Nurses carried off the precious marrow to be tested. We sat in a small white room and twiddled our thumbs, made small talk, prayed, joked about the insanity of it all.

Under the microscope, leukemia cells are obvious. Red blood cells are round and red like little balloons and have the job of giving us pep and energy. The white cells that protect us from infection are white and look uniform and intentional. Leukemia cells are bigger and come in multiple shapes and colors—purples, yellows or even multicolored. Some have six or eight legs of different lengths. They're all different, but they all look wrong, evil.

So, together, Dr. Dan and I told Kristal that she had cancer of the blood. He did the technical doctor stuff, and I did the you'll-be-okay mother stuff.

Finally, the medical people all left the room. Right away, Kristal wanted to call her dad. Funny. She hadn't seen him for months, yet in a time of crisis, she wanted him close. Gary and I had been divorced since she was four. He lived only an hour from us, but these days they usually only got together for family weddings or special events. I found a phone and called him. He said he'd be right there and hung up.

While they prepared a room for Kristal upstairs, she and I wandered around the hospital, getting our first look at what would soon feel like our own home. We had begun attending church a few months earlier, so we were delighted to find a tiny chapel with stained glass windows and three short pews. Up front, a spindly podium held an enormous Bible in mid-air, reminding me of a skinny little person with giant open arms.

This place felt safe and comforting.

"What about my hair?" Kristal said, finally feeling the freedom to break down. She fell into my arms. "The doctor said I may lose it. What if I go bald?"

She was thinking about her hair. Only her hair. It hadn't occurred to her that she would be very sick, that she could lose her very life. Of course she had no context. She had never known illness, never known anyone who died of this disease or any other.

I, on the other hand, knew a little about leukemia. In fact, the girl I knew who had died of it had been Kristal's babysitter when she was a toddler. Now my daughter had the same awful stuff. And I knew I couldn't protect her, couldn't prevent the pain or heartache that was certain to eat its voracious way into her path. I had never felt so lonely and alone.

My feeling of helplessness was as big as all outdoors.

But in this tiny chapel, we could hold each other and cry with no one watching, Kristal about her hair, me about her pain. That's where Gary found us. The door banged open and he stormed in. Blond, big-shouldered and big-mouthed too.

"Well, I don't know what the hell you're doin' in here!" he yelled, alcohol on his breath.

He grabbed Kristal and held her for a moment, then pushed her back and held her at arm's length.

"Tell me what the doctors are saying."

In tandem, Kristal and I recapped what we'd heard so far. When she got to the part about maybe losing her hair, she started crying all over again.

"Your hair???" he boomed. "Is that what you're so upset about? Your hair? That's just ridiculous!"

As he berated her, she continued to cry. Soon he left to find the doctor and get the whole story. Kristal said she wished she'd never called him.

That was the beginning of our 20-month ordeal. Kristal

had gone into remission twice, relapsed twice. Finally the once-effective chemotherapy, which left her so nauseous and twice caused her sandy blonde hair to fall out, no longer worked. This third time, Dr. Dan had sent his colleague to tell us there was no hope. I imagined them tossing a coin to decide who had to deliver news like this to parents.

Kristal and I, together, made the decision not to continue treatment. Her chart now said, "No heroics." In permanent ink.

2
HOW'D I GET HERE?

Chronologically, I was 20 years old when I got married, but in the ways of the world, I was such a babe. Gary had run-your-fingers-through-it blond hair, blue eyes, a thin waist and hunky wide shoulders. He was handsome in a Joe Namath sort of way. A friend introduced me to him while he was still recuperating from bits of shrapnel that exploded into his leg as he dove into a bunker in Vietnam. I was smitten.

The boys I'd dated up to this point had taken me to McDonald's. Gary introduced me to restaurants with multiple forks. He called when he said he would. He opened car doors for me. Other than my favorite grandmother, he was the first person in my life who listened to what I thought. He even stopped at my house on his way home from work to leave romantic notes on my windshield.

And I immediately loved Gary's mother, Henrietta. She was the total opposite of my mother. The first time I met her, she threw her arms around me in a bear hug of a welcome. She laughed out loud. We had just spent nearly two hours in the car but ten minutes after we arrived at her house, Henrietta and Gary decided that the sunshine deserved to be celebrated by driving another 50 miles to the Washington coast.

She swung easily into the back seat of Gary's little yellow Toyota and we raced off. She and Gary were both drinking beer. But the real kicker was a half hour later. She suddenly sprang up in the space between the front seats and yelled, "Stop the car! Stop the car! I've gotta pee." My mother would NEVER have done that.

As if they'd done this a thousand times, Gary whipped the car to the side of the country road. Henrietta hopped out and ran into the bushes. I don't think my mouth closed properly until she was safely back in the car. With Henrietta, what you saw was what you got. She was real. Honest. Straightforward. And her feet were size 10s, just like mine. We got along well from the first.

As soon as her first grandchild was born, Henrietta became Grandma Hennie. She was the kind of grandma who played, the kind who rolled around on the floor with her grandkids. I had heard that Dutch people were stern, but Grandma Hennie was full of fun.

And she spoiled Kristal, of course. Got her anything she wanted. Bought her candy and Twinkies and all the other stuff I wouldn't. Once, when Kristal was a toddler, we all went to a Chinese restaurant for lunch. Kristal wanted some of the barbequed pork we were eating. I chopped up some and put it on her highchair. But that wasn't enough. She wanted it dipped in hot mustard. I kept telling her it was hot and she wouldn't like it, but she kept whining about it.

"Okaaay," I said after the fourth time. "You asked for it."

I dipped a piece in the mustard and handed it to her, knowing full well that she'd cry when it stung her tongue and cleaned out her sinuses. But I also knew it wouldn't hurt her, so in the hope that she wouldn't argue the next time I said no, I handed it to her anyway.

Well, you know what happened, right? The millisecond that hot mustard hit her tongue, her eyes bugged out like a cartoon character. She screamed like I had shoved a hot poker down her throat. While I shrugged my shoulders and said, "I told you so," Grandma Hennie whipped her out of the high chair and patted her until she calmed down.

Grandma Hennie let her do other things as well. Instead of her pajamas, Grandma let Kristal wear sunglasses and

Grandpa's old Budweiser T-shirt to bed. Kristal loved going to her Grandma's, even though it meant two hours on twisting, country roads.

The first time she visited for the weekend without me, Kristal was about 4. This was before child seats were commonly used, and Henrietta made the mistake of putting Kristal beside her on the front seat. Between them sat Henrietta's big old black bucket of a purse—the kind with an open zippered top and lots of sections for LifeSavers and gum and Band Aids and safety pins and anything else a proper grandma might need.

Unfortunately, Henrietta wasn't as practiced at pulling over as Gary was. So when Kristal said she was sick, Henrietta didn't even ALMOST make it. Kristal hit the purse dead center. Made a big mess, all over everything that Grandma needed. Well, except for the roll of paper towels and Lysol that she didn't have with her.

Afterwards, they took turns telling me how stinky it was the rest of the way home, cracking up all the while. These two were a force to be reckoned with.

But I'm getting ahead of myself. When Gary asked me to marry him after only three months, I envisioned setting a pretty table and having candlelight dinners with my adoring husband every night. What I didn't know until after we were married was that he was in a lot of pain. That he was an alcoholic. That he often didn't come home at night until the bar closed. Soon, my entire body tensed up when I heard his green VW van pull into the driveway.

Gary was an impressive guy, no doubt about it. When I introduced him to people, they asked one of two things— either, "Wow, where did you find this guy? He's a prince!" or "Where did you find that asshole?" It depended upon whether or not he'd been drinking.

Life with Gary could be like a cheap carnival ride. Sometimes I'd crawl onto a ride that looked safe only to be surprised when my head started whipping back and forth. But once in a while during our four-year marriage, that sweet guy I thought I married would show up again. One Thanksgiving, for instance, he surprised me with a new stove, then stayed up until three in the morning stripping the wax buildup he found under the old one. But on Sundays during football season, his twelve-pack didn't even get warm beside his recliner while he watched football games.

This was not what I'd expected marriage to be. Instead of romantic dinners I got toasted cheese sandwiches and a can of soup with a toddler. Yes, I was married, but I felt very alone. I knew I was totally responsible for the house and my child. I soon learned that I couldn't count on Gary or anyone else to help. Some days I would have sold my soul for the chance to take a nice hot bath in peace and quiet.

"Don't make me any promises you can't keep," became my most-often-repeated saying.

But when I complained that Gary was late or he'd cancelled another plan to take us on a picnic or to the zoo, Gary wasn't there to listen and Kristal was usually the only one who heard me. Today they call unloading on your child emotional abuse, but in the '70s, I had no idea it was inappropriate. I just knew I was mad as hell and needed to yell about it once in a while—which, in retrospect, could be why he never came home.

Even when she was little, Kristal wouldn't hear complaints about her father. She defended him to the end. If I mentioned that he must be stuck on a barstool somewhere AGAIN and that he didn't care about us, she rose up like a little pink lawyer.

"Oh, I know my Daddy loves me," she said, her spindly blonde pigtails bobbing defiantly.

"How would you know that?" I challenged. "He's never here!"

"Because every morning when I get up, there's a piece

of beef jerky at my place at the table. He always thinks of me when he's at the tavern."

All the air left my lungs when she said that. What could I say?

The first time Gary hit me, I knew it was time for him to leave. It was only a slug in the arm and Gary said it was an accident, but it pushed me into a decision I'd put off for too long. Kristal was 4. She wailed and cried when he left, but suddenly our house was more peaceful than it had been for years. Gary moved in with some girl within the week. I was working part-time at J.C. Penney's, and my house payment (in 1974) was a whopping $105 a month. I didn't know if I could afford it, so Laurie, a co-worker from the shoe department, moved in for a few months to help with the expenses.

Kristal saw her dad on Sundays—at first. But as the weeks went on, he arrived later and later. It broke my heart to see her standing there, nose pressed against the leaded glass of the front door. After a while, she'd collapse into her favorite chair, her little red suitcase standing at attention beside her. Sometimes she mercifully fell asleep.

One day, after hours of nose pressing, she asked, "Why can't I make my daddy love me?"

How stupid, I thought, for a father to put his ex-wife in the position of defending him. "He must've gotten busy" or "He gets distracted," I offered. I tried to spare Kristal's feelings, but five years of lame excuses had made her wise beyond her years.

What Gary didn't understand is that to a child, time and love are the same thing.

In those days, even when we had no money, Kristal and I spent our spare time at the mall. We didn't buy much but we loved window-shopping. Dreaming was cheap and we spent a lot of time planning what we'd buy when we could afford it. I moved on to a job auditing 7-Eleven stores, but we still spent most Saturdays dreaming about spending money rather than actually doing it.

One Saturday when she was in kindergarten, Kristal asked if she could get her ears pierced. The best part about being a single mom is making decisions without having to consult anyone. And the spontaneity. I loved that part too.

"Sure," I said with a shrug.

"Okay, let's go to the mall," she said. We hopped in the car and off we went. When she saw the jeweler's piercing device—which looked a lot like a gun—my gutsy little girl had second thoughts.

"You go first," she said with a giggle. "Then I'll do it."

I rolled my eyes and laughed. I'd been thinking about piercing my ears for years but just never got around to it, so I said okay. It stung a little but I tried to keep my face straight so she wouldn't notice. But Kristal never missed anything. She'd seen me wince. No matter what I or the saleslady said, she wouldn't come near that piercing machine. Aaaugh. Motherhood. I drove home with holes in my ears and a cute new pair of silver earrings in my bag. She went home with her ears intact.

The next week, the little charmer had to talk a little harder to get me to the mall. At the Bon, as I searched through the markdown rack, she grabbed my arm.

"Now. We've got to go now," she said, sounding like she was doing her bathroom dance. "I'm ready right now."

"Okay, okay," I said, as she dragged me away from a darling blouse the color of a Hawaiian lagoon.

The jeweler nodded knowingly when we walked in the door. Talking softly, she helped Kristal onto the stool and painted a little dot on her earlobes. When the gun went off, Kristal's chin began to quiver, then her entire face collapsed.

"Aaauuh," she sobbed. It took a few minutes but she was soon ready to do the other ear. When the lady cocked the gun, Kristal squeezed my hand as hard as she could. At the time, I had no idea how many times we'd use that hand-squeezing trick in the years to come. When her ears were pierced that day, I bought her a cute pair of earrings too.

So, why didn't I just look for another guy to replace Gary? It would have been great to have help with the bills, help with the parenting and someone to snuggle with at night. But I was gun-shy. I'd fallen so hard for Gary, who proved to be totally different than I had thought. He was the only man I'd ever slept with. I didn't trust my instincts as far as men were concerned. And I didn't trust men. They were not what they appeared to be, and I no longer believed a word they said.

Besides, I was exhausted when I got home from work. I didn't have the energy or the money for babysitters while I went out. And where would I have gone? Out drinking? I knew better than to try to find a reliable, responsible guy in a bar. Nah. I was convinced that single parenthood was my fault and my problem.

After a couple of years of working to keep food on the table, I had traded up a bit job-wise. I cranked up my courage and decided to go after something better. It was the 70s, after all, and the world was changing. Women's Lib had given me options I would never have dreamed of and I decided to aim high.

As an auditor, I inventoried a different 7-Eleven store every day. For more than a year I'd been watching the truck drivers deliver bread, beer, pop and such. Noting the effort involved in each man's job, I decided that chips were the easiest to deliver since they weighed considerably less than Wonder Bread, Budweiser or Pepsi. One day I was telling a store owner about my plan to move up in the world when a Frito truck drove up and two guys piled out.

"Why don't you ask HIM for a job?" the owner asked just as the men passed right in front of us.

"Okay," I said, playing along. I had nothing to lose,

right?

"How about a job?" I said to one of the guys. He stopped and looked at me while the other one hustled over to the chip rack.

"Haaa!" he scoffed. "We don't hire women!"

"Well, that's dumb. Why not?" I shot back.

"Well—you know—they get sick, they get their periods, they quit..."

"Not me," I said. "I'm healthy as a horse, and I've spent years in every one of my jobs."

He continued to walk around the store while I worked in one aisle. Every time he passed by, he gave me another reason why hiring women was a ridiculous idea.

"We have 27 men in our warehouse. You couldn't stand the language."

"Shiiitttt," I drew out the word and tossed it over my shoulder. "I can cuss with the best of them."

"Women get pregnant and quit," he said on the next pass.

"Not me. I was just divorced and I've had enough of men." That sure was true.

Fifteen minutes later the other man finished stocking shelves and he and the argumentative one were ready to leave. He walked my way one more time.

"If you're really serious," he said, handing me a business card, "call me. We're going to need a couple of relief drivers soon."

"Okay," I said. It wasn't until after he left that I read his card. District Manager, it said. Gulp. If I'd had any idea who he was I would never have been so gutsy.

Kristal was horrified at the very idea of me being a truck driver. "But that's a MAN'S job," she said with her hands on her teeny hips. Have I mentioned that the girl never even got dirty? Mud pies? Not Kristal. She'd come in after playing in the back yard, hold out her hands as if they were full of poo, then head for the bathroom to wash up. My daughter was a total girl—the first time she ripped a hole in the knee of her jeans, she was in third grade.

"Kristal Lynn!" I said when I saw the rip. "Look at your jeans! What happened?"

She brightened. "Isn't it cool? I've been trying to do this for years!"

Anyway, before I took that truck driver job, Kristal had a limited view of womanhood, just as I had at her age. I knew she needed to hear about my dad's Aunt Maylou.

When I was a little girl, I began, every woman I knew matched the same description. She was a housewife and mother, she spent her days cleaning to keep her house neat and canning to keep food on the table, she called her husband Dear, and wore a cotton calico print housedress that buttoned at the bodice and gathered at the waist. After all, it was the 50s in South Dakota.

But when I was about six, I met Aunt Maylou, who totally revised my view of women. My dad sometimes talked about this aunt, but since she didn't live within a 15-mile radius like his parents, siblings, cousins, aunts and uncles, I'd never met her. One Saturday mom made all four of us kids put on our Sunday best. In the heat of a South Dakota summer, we piled in the car and drove a couple of hours to Mobridge, where Aunt Maylou lived. There, the streets were lined with shade trees, the houses were freshly painted and the yards neatly trimmed.

Whoa, she must be rich, I thought as we pulled up to a tall white house with pillars and a porch that wrapped all the way around. I quickly pulled on the white gloves mom handed us.

We piled out of the car and lined up on the porch like little ducklings. The woman who opened the door looked like every other woman I knew. Hair pulled up, dirndl skirt, sensible shoes. But she turned and called over her shoulder,

"Maylou, your family is here." My sisters glanced at each other and giggled. Aunt Maylou had a maid!

We stood in an immaculate parlor with high ceilings and as many bookshelves as our small town public library. We heard Aunt Maylou before we saw her. The click, click, click of high heels on shining wood floors echoed in the hall. Aunt Maylou appeared in a two-piece suit the color of the green on a mallard duck's neck. Her gray hair was up in some sort of fancy twist, and she wore a big shiny broach on her lapel. On a Saturday! I'd never seen anyone who looked so distinguished.

My dad enfolded her in one of his big hugs and lifted her off the ground. She squealed with delight and turned to meet all of us. In size order, she shook our hands and looked us right in the eye and smiled a big warm smile. Her eyes twinkled as she asked us each a question, then waited to listen to our answers. I was enthralled. I got the sense that she really liked her life and who she was.

I had trouble keeping my eyes in my head as she showed us around. Everywhere in the house, things sparkled and shined and made noises I'd never heard. A grandfather clock chimed and a clock coo-cooed in the hallway. The dining table was set with sparkling crystal and china. Maybe she saw how nervous I was just thinking about having to eat there, because she said we were going to the diner for lunch. Again with the little duckling grouping, we walked downtown. Something else amazed me, I told Kristal, who sat enraptured by the story of her great, great aunt.

Every single person we met along the way tipped their hats and said, "Good morning, Maylou" or "I see you have company, Maylou" or "Nice day we're having" or something. Even the children stopped their bikes to say hello. They all knew her name. She must be somebody really important, I thought. She even introduced us to people—like she was proud of us, like WE were somebody too.

By listening to every word she said over the club

sandwich my sister and I shared, I found out that Aunt Maylou and her husband owned the local drug store. It was like she was the Mayor of the whole town! She was also on the Board for the University and had all kinds of other important responsibilities. A woman! Go figure.

"Maylou was like no one I'd ever met," I explained to Kristal. "She not only got to make her own decisions, but she made rules for other people too. I felt like royalty just knowing this charming woman with the twinkling eyes.

"That morning, Maylou opened my mind. Women didn't have to wear gathered skirts. Women could own businesses. Women could be mayors. Women could be sweet and kind and lovely, even to children. Women could be happy."

Kristal nodded. Along with a quick explanation of the raise I'd get in salary and the difference between window-shopping and actual shopping, she agreed that I should go after the truck-driving job.

So, after cranking up my courage several more times through a series of phone calls and interviews, I became the first female truck driver Frito-Lay ever hired, at least in Washington State.

I loved the job, loved watching people's jaws drop when I artfully dipped a hand truck with a seven-foot stack of boxes through the automatic doors of a grocery store or zipped effortlessly into a parallel parking spot. I also loved the Teamster's benefits—insurance, paid vacations and an income we could easily live on. Finally, I was proud of myself, beholden to no one, independent and self-sufficient. It gave me a confidence that made me a better mother. With my own money, I didn't need anyone to ride in on a white horse to save me.

But Kristal and I didn't have as much time together as we used to. Because I had to load my truck at 6 A.M., I had to carry my sleeping daughter across the alley to her best friend Tina's house. I deposited her and the outfit we'd picked out the night before on the couch. Tina's mom got the girls up, fed them breakfast and walked them to school. If I wasn't home when she returned from school, she and Tina played Barbies or watched cartoons until I arrived. I sometimes felt guilty, but she seemed to love more time to play with her friend.

The job was hard work but after a few months of intense physical labor, I was in the best shape of my life. My hair was long and blonde, and I tossed it like Farrah Fawcett. After being chunky for most of my life, I looked good and I knew it. I was 26 and independent, 36-24-36, but my heart was getting harder by the day.

And, oh mama, did I learn to cuss with the best of them! I spent my days smack dab in the middle of a pack of men. I saw a side of them I'd never seen before. I heard them complain about their ex-wives squandering their hard-earned child support, heard the way they spoke (at least on the phone) to the wives they had. Maybe they were just bragging, but I heard them talk about their escapades when their wives weren't around. It wasn't pretty. From the way they talked, I could count the faithful ones on the fingers of my hands. The worst part of it was that their behavior became normal to me, and I became like them in more ways than I care to admit.

After four years, I grew weary of this lifestyle. I wanted another baby, wanted to be married. By this time I was two years into a relationship with Jerry, one of the men I worked with. He was kind, worked hard and had some ambition, plus he was 6'4", which made me feel feminine for a change. Jerry wasn't a drinker, but he bought a tavern and after working eight hours on a truck, he had a nap, then did a night shift there. It was a grueling schedule. He had a young son, Brian, from his previous marriage, which had ended because he'd been unfaithful. It sounded like he had learned his lesson. I married him, then found out I was dead wrong.

Over our eight-year marriage, I knew about six or eight of his girlfriends, mostly barmaids. But the knowing was limited to the recesses of my mind. I didn't say it out loud. Didn't talk to him about it. Didn't even admit it to myself. Because the day I faced it head on, I knew I'd have to do something about it. Strange. It wasn't until after I began to seek God that I discovered I needed to live in truth. That caused me to finally admit to myself that those women were real.

In Jerry's defense, he looked a whole lot better to the women who frequented his tavern than the drunk on the next barstool. This guy was a former basketball star and owned the place, after all, which made him a magnet for barflies. He wasn't confident or outgoing enough to mastermind these liaisons; he just couldn't say no. Come to think of it, Jerry didn't say much of anything.

For the first few years, we had had fun together. We took the kids camping and out in his boat. Brian was three years younger than Kristal, and they got along like siblings, riding bikes, singing and putting on plays on the deck. Although Kristal and Jerry weren't particularly close, I convinced myself that would change with time and we got married anyway. I was ready for another baby.

Jerry and I talked about it—one sentence I think— beforehand. About six months into the marriage, I mentioned one night that I thought it was time to have a baby. After what seemed like a long time of holding my breath there in the dark, he simply said, "Okay," then fell asleep.

It had taken Jerry's first wife years to get pregnant, so his frame of reference was different than mine. Kristal had been conceived after only three tries. As an incredibly naïve 20-year-old, this had come as something of a surprise to me. The first time around. Not the second.

Within a month of Jerry's one-line approval, I was throwing up when I poured the coffee into the pot in the mornings. I was too excited for words. I don't think he said anything either. Kristal, on the other hand, was over the moon about it.

Jerry had bought another tavern and quit his job at Frito. Soon afterward, he talked me into leaving my well-paid Teamster job so I could help him. I began running the kitchen at the new tavern, the Floatation Device. (And yes, in case you're wondering, I had consulted a dictionary before we named it that. I was convinced that Webster had mistakenly left out the "a." The word float clearly had an "a," so should flotation, I reasoned.)

We had a regular weekday crowd at the tavern—sheet rockers, plumbers and local Joes. I went in to prepare workingmen's favorites like chili, spaghetti and meat loaf for the daily lunch special. I specialized in big, fat, juicy burgers that dripped down your arm. Pregnancy caused me to make just two adjustments to my regular culinary activities—someone else had to make the coffee and chop the onions.

I stayed at the tavern until the lunch rush was over and then left in time to be there when Kristal got home from school. At the time, my friend Madge and I co-coached Kristal's third/fourth grade softball team. We had a great time doing it, but neither Madge nor I could make the girls serious about softball.

Girls at that age draw circles in the dirt, we found. They pick the flowers in left field. They don't, however, care much about the sport for which we moms are forking over perfectly good money for fees and uniforms. Why, I remember at the last game of the season, with my own daughter on second base, I yelled to remind her, "Don't run on a fly!"

"What's a fly?" the little darling yelled back. Hopeless.

One day, about nine weeks into my pregnancy, after running around the field with the girls, I started bleeding. Just a little. I didn't give it another thought—until it happened again the next week.

"Don't worry," friends advised. "Lots of women spot, sometimes all the way through their pregnancies."

But it continued. I finally called the doctor one Tuesday morning while dicing potatoes for clam chowder.

"Go home," he ordered, scaring me. "Lie flat on your back and stay that way. Complete bed rest may save this pregnancy."

I told Jerry. He didn't take the news well, didn't want to listen to my fears about losing this child I was already naming. I was determined to do whatever I could to save my baby's life.

"So who's going to handle the kitchen?" he said, as close to yelling as he ever got.

"I guess you are," I said, grabbing my purse.

"It's 11 o'clock now. You've got to at least stay through lunch."

"Sorry, I can't. Doctor's orders. I've got to go," I said, heading out the back door.

When Kristal heard the news, she was worried. She'd been asking for a sister for years and didn't want anything to happen to this baby. She fetched whatever I needed and fixed a little tea party for us on the couch. When we watched *Little House on the Prairie* that day, I'm not sure whether I was holding her or she was holding me.

Jerry did not understand the concept of bed rest. When he got home he was genuinely surprised not to find dinner on the table. The next day he was surprised again. More than once he mentioned that the floor needed vacuuming. Finally he got disgusted enough and did it himself. I was still hoping that if I did what the doctor recommended, the bleeding would stop and our baby would be fine.

"And what about the tavern convention this weekend?" he asked. "I suppose you're not going to that either. I've already paid for it, you know."

"If the bleeding stops then I could probably still go," I said, partly to appease him and partly to reassure myself.

But the bleeding increased. The worse it got, the more

I feared that I would never hold this child, never see him take his first steps, never send him off to kindergarten. On Friday, Jerry complained that he had to go to the conference alone and left. I didn't hear from him all weekend.

On Saturday, my old roommate Laurie from J.C. Penney's came over and cried with me. She scrubbed the kitchen floor, did a couple of loads of laundry and fixed us a nice dinner. The bleeding had gotten as bad as a heavy period and then the cramping began. Laurie left to care for her own family and Kristal went to bed. I was alone. The cramping became harder and harder. I cried like I have never cried before and finally accepted the inevitable. There was no way my child could survive this.

All night I was up with intense cramps and bleeding. I was losing blood clots that looked like hunks of liver, but I didn't want to bother anyone in this embarrassing condition, so I didn't call 911 or my doctor. I sat on the toilet, a permanent circle on my backside, no longer even trying to get back to the couch because I couldn't make it there and back before my clothes were bloodied. For hours, I shivered with cold, dread and grief. I have never felt so lonely. I kept imagining Kristal finding me in the morning, lying in a pool of blood on that awful pink-tiled bathroom floor. She was too young to live without her mom.

Who, I wondered, would take care of her? Not Jerry. After we married, she began using his last name on her school papers. But after only three months, it became apparent that he was not the father figure she had hoped for, so she changed her name back. Gary? Maybe, but I didn't even want to think about that.

Instead, I got down on my hands and knees, trying to scrub bloodstains out of the grout. Kristal, I determined, might find me dead, but she sure as heck wasn't going to find any pool of blood.

By 4 A.M., the cramping eased and the bleeding

slowed. I knew it was over. My baby was gone. I had cried until I could cry no more. I felt hollow and empty. Finally, I slept.

Kristal did find me in the morning. I probably looked dead, but I was actually only exhausted. She crawled into bed with me, and we cried together when I told her the baby was gone. We read books and fell back to sleep. She quietly fixed us cereal, then soup and sandwiches for lunch, each time making a big deal of setting the coffee table for our meal. Jerry arrived at around 5 o'clock that afternoon and told me a little about the convention. I waited, but he didn't ask about the baby.

When I had called the doctor's service early that morning, they said that I should probably just come in for my scheduled appointment on Monday. I finally told Jerry and asked him to go with me, but he had a lot to do since he'd been away from the business all weekend. So I dried my tears, thrust my chin in the air and walked in to the doctor's office alone.

I did okay in the waiting room with all those heavy-bellied women . . . until a mother with adorable twins showed up for her postpartum checkup. A kind nurse guided me into an exam room while I tried to pull myself back together.

The doctor, an ex-military man, came in while I was still crying.

"I don't know what you're cryin' about," he said with all the emotion of the iceberg that brought down the Titanic. "Did you really want this baby?"

There are some things a woman should never have to bear, and I knew I had just experienced one of them. I got out of that man's office as quickly as I could. If I'd had the courage of a flea, I would have emptied his bio-hazardous waste container over his head on my way out.

But then, I thought, why should a perfect stranger be any more caring than my own husband? As far as I was concerned, I was done with men.

3
FINDING FAITH

But three months after my miscarriage I was pregnant again. Never did take me long. Being pregnant at 21 had been a joyful walk in the park. This time I felt like I was covering the same ground with insomnia, a broken leg and severe arthritis. Mostly I was just exhausted, especially after preparing and serving lunch for 100 or more. By the time I got home to meet Kristal after school, all I could do was collapse on the couch.

Sometimes I brought home a pizza or fried chicken from work because I didn't have the energy to cook dinner. Kristal began playing waitress when she was 5 and at nearly 10, she still loved serving. She'd stick our dinner in the microwave or make a sandwich and deliver it like a waitress looking for a big fat tip. We'd sit, she in her favorite velour chair, and watch *Little House on the Prairie* together. Jerry usually worked late.

We painted the baby's bedroom bright blue on the bottom and white on the top, then installed a yellow border in the middle. Kristal was not nuts about the idea of giving up the bedroom across the hall from ours to move to the first floor of our daylight basement house. She didn't mind it when Brian was with us for the weekend, but Kristal was nervous to be so far from us the rest of the time. I pushed the advantages of having her own private bathroom and being close to the jukebox and pool table. Let's face it, she didn't play pool. But after helping to choose a bigger bed, bedding and drapes, she warmed up to the idea.

But the day Kristal saw a mouse run across the floor downstairs, she was petrified all over again. Jerry called her a scaredy-cat and insisted she sleep in her room. We put out a few mousetraps to catch the little critter. Meanwhile, I told her that mice were WAY more afraid of her than she was of them, and suggested she let them know she was coming by making some noise as she went down the stairs. But the first time she tried it, I threw back my head and laughed.

"Beep," she said in a staccato voice, stomping her way down the steps. "Beep. Beep-beep. Beep." Years later, she told me she'd once spent the night sleeping on the top of the steps.

Soon it was time to put the crib together. So one Saturday, I dumped all the parts onto the living room floor. Then the fun began. Bolts and screwdrivers are not my strength and although the kids handed me tools, they were not a whole lot of help. After a few hours of celebrating when some piece fit where it was supposed to and cussing when it didn't, the danged thing looked like it could indeed safely hold a baby. Kristal, Brian, and I paraded it through the hallway, pushing it on its newly installed wheels, into the baby's new bedroom.

But when we approached, I knew we were in trouble. The crib was wider than the bedroom door. I didn't take it well. Shook my head and wondered when my life would begin to go right. Stomped and screamed. I wish I'd been thinking about the example I was setting.

My lack of support was frustrating. As much as I wanted someone to burst through the door and rescue me, I knew no one was coming. Didn't see many choices. Didn't yet know I could call on God. This was my responsibility. My mother often said, "You have made your bed. Now lie in it." This bed sagged in the middle, had springs sticking out and bedbugs to boot.

I knew I had to do what moms have been doing since

the beginning of time—be the responsible adult. I took the crib apart again, shoved it into the bedroom and started over. I wish I could say that was the only time I struggled with being alone, even while I was married.

One particularly trying day when I was feeling no support and my hormones were racing through my veins so fast that they were probably visible right through my blouse, I got in the car and drove. No destination—just a sobbing, get-out-of-the-house sort of drive. I ended up on a dead end road on the edge of the winter woods. I sat there in the car on a drippy Northwest day, crying and complaining about my sorry situation.

I feel so alone. Jerry doesn't even care about this child I'm carrying! It's his baby too! Will he help or will I have to raise it alone? It's not fair! Dads are supposed to help! My dad always did.

Sitting there watching the windows steam up, I caught a glimpse of a busy little squirrel running from branch to branch. She hurried like a mother trying to bring home the bacon. I watched her until I could hardly see out the windows, wondering what motherhood must be like for her. While her babies' daddy ran after the next squirrel in heat, she raised the children alone. Gathered nuts alone. I'd seen TV shows that showed squalling, hungry babies in their nests. That's what the poor thing faced every time she stuck her head in the front door. And all over the woods, little squirrel mamas were in the same boat.

My mind ticked through the rest of the animal world. *What does life look like to a mama deer?* I wondered. *A cow or a whale or a cheetah?* Penguins and seahorses seemed more evolved in the area of parenthood, but for the most part, I realized that animal mothers raised children alone! In their world, after a long chase to win the female and a few minutes of sex in the bush, the males left—totally satisfied with their part in the deal.

But after that one short encounter, the females were left pregnant. And as wonderful as children are, they sometimes leave mothers feeling stuck. Just like me in this car. I wondered if animals minded taking total responsibility to provide and care for their children. Did they know any better? Mother bears deliver their cubs in a den and have to protect them—even from their fathers. And lionesses not only have to provide for their little ones, but chase down dinner for the big bellowing males too! At least I didn't have to hunt for my dinner.

Something clicked, like a coin dropping. Over in the corner of my mind, I heard a little voice. Not out loud, but more like a conscience.

"The females of this world carry the children," I heard. "They have the responsibilities, yes, but I have also given them all they need to raise their families: wisdom, giving hearts and a fierce love for their children. I'll do the same for you."

Suddenly, I let out a deep sigh and a sense of peace came over me. It took me years to realize that what I had heard was God's voice. He was promising me that I was never really alone and that He'd be right there beside me.

That day, I developed a theory—squirrels are sometimes pickier than women at choosing mates. At least they wait for the mightiest, most persistent squirrel in the forest. The same cannot always be said of women. Of me.

Kristal was nearly 10 when Jeff was born. When I called her school from the hospital to tell her that he had arrived, the office attendant ran down to her classroom to get her.

"Hey, Kristal! Guess what! It's a boy!" I said from the maternity ward when she picked up the phone.

"Awww, Mommm," she drew out. "I really wanted a girl!" But she melted when she met her little brother. Well, at 9 pounds, 11 ounces, he wasn't so little, but Kristal loved having a baby in the house.

If I hadn't nursed Jeff, I probably wouldn't have seen the child for the first six months. Whenever he slept, Kristal waited attentively for him to wake up. As soon as he made the slightest little coo from his crib, Kristal ran to his room.

"I'll get him! I'll get him!" she'd say, already bounding off to rescue him from his dreaded nap. I had wondered if I'd like having a boy, since I didn't fully appreciate dirt and bugs and lizards. Luckily, this one reached out with one baby finger and grabbed hold of my heart. I even loved his tiny John Deere tractors and tools. Loved listening to him make truck noises as he zoomed them around the living room. Sons are a wonder too, I decided.

We took him on his first camping trip at six weeks. Even as a baby, he especially loved boating. A couple of times a week during the summer, I'd pack up our dinner to eat picnic-style on the boat. Jerry and I loved to swim, water ski and fish; Kristal and Brian sang and danced for us in the back of the boat.

When Jeff was just over a year old, I tried to find one of those baby gates so he wouldn't fall down the stairs. Couldn't find one in the whole town.

"I couldn't even find Jeff a pair of overalls for under $25!" I told Jerry that night. What this town needs is a children's clothing store! Someone needs to open a place where people could find cute stuff—even for boys—at reasonable prices."

"Okay," he said, nodding as if people made these enormous decisions every day. "Why don't you open one? You go look for a location and I'll go see about a loan."

Over the last several months he'd been asking when I was going back to work, mentioning things like "pulling your own weight around here," so I shouldn't have been surprised.

But the more I thought about the idea of a store, the more I loved the idea. As a teenager, I'd worked as an assistant buyer for a department store so I knew about buying and selling. Since it was a kid's store, I thought I could take Jeff to work with me so I found a great spot in a new shopping center that had big plans for expansion.

Jerry had a good sense of business, a terrific work ethic and seemed to instinctively know what would work and what wouldn't. He co-signed a loan for $25,000 to get me started.

I thought a lot about what to name the store. Shirley's? Yuck. Egotistical, or at least unimaginative. Kid's clothes? Too obvious. I needed a name that said children without using the word children. It came to me while gardening one day. Trowel in hand, the word *bubblegum* popped into my mind! And what said clothing more than *closet?* So, my store became the Bubblegum Closet. I called a graphic artist, decided on an old-fashioned bubblegum machine as a logo, ordered a sign and I was ready.

Within four months, I was open for business. Jeff was 18 months old and played happily in the big play corner I'd stocked with toys like trucks, teddy bears and typewriters. At first. But he soon got bored and tried to climb on me when I was with a customer. Or someone asked for a smaller size when I was changing a diaper. I soon realized that I couldn't be a good mom and a businesswoman—at least not simultaneously. For my sanity and Jeff's too, I had to separate the two into different portions of my day.

So I put an ad in the paper and found Alice—THE most wonderful grandma-type lady on our rural little Fox island. She came to our waterfront house to watch Jeff, which allowed him to nap in his own bed and play with his own toys. She potty-trained him in nothing flat. That first week, she called me at work. Scared me. I thought Jeff must have fallen or be bleeding somewhere.

"I see that you have some laundry in the hamper," she said casually. "Would you like me to throw it into the washing machine for you?"

"Whaat?" I stammered, knowing that the basket was overflowing. "You want to help with the laundry?"

"Sure. Since I'm here all day, I've got time. It would give me something to do when Jeff is napping."

If she'd have been closer, I probably would have picked up and twirled her in the air! Within the first few weeks, she also offered to do some ironing, put the roast in the oven for dinner and asked if she could bake a cake. She introduced Jeff to chocolate cake with peanut butter frosting, (look for the recipe at www.kristalswedding.com) which is still a mandatory part of every Walston birthday.

Because Alice was there when Kristal got home from school, I could work until 6:00 every night without worrying about her. Better than that, I came home every night to find dinner on the table and the house sparkling. Alice became my housewife. After a couple of exhausting months, my life was sooo much easier. I can certainly see why men love having someone at home taking care of everything. It was heaven.

So when did I get to the point of calling on God? It was a slow process. I grew up going to church every Sunday. We were at church whenever the place was open. My father was a deacon and Sunday school Superintendent at a Lutheran church in Seattle. At every pancake breakfast during my growing up years, I remember him in the basement kitchen, surrounded by the women of the church, cracking jokes in his white apron. He flipped more pancakes than any of the other dads, probably because he always made them for us kids on weekends so Mom could sleep in.

Once, several of us big shot sixth graders were messing around in the Sanctuary during a Sunday night potluck when someone—I think it was a kid named Jeff who our Sunday school teacher always called "the little dickens"—hushed us and said, "See that red candle on the altar? It's the eternal flame. It came all the way from Jerusalem. It can't ever be blown out."

"Can too," I scoffed. There must have been something in my mother's sausage and rice casserole that night, because at that age I was rarely brave enough to have said something like that. Anyway, now I had all the other kids' attention, so I went on.

"It's only a candle. Anybody can blow out a candle."

"Huh-uh," Jeff said with attitude. "It means the Holy Spirit is here. No one can ever blow it out. Even a big wind couldn't blow it out."

"Well, they might say that, but it's just a plain old candle."

"Blow it out then," Jeff challenged, arms folded across his chest.

Now who, I ask you, could resist a double dog dare like that? Knees shaking under my calico print skirt, I walked up to the altar, took a deep breath, and blew the thing out. One little puff was all it took.

"See?" I said simply.

Behind me, I heard scampering. Everyone scattered, and I stood there on the altar alone. With the eternal flame out and me responsible, I felt a chill right down my spine, as if that little flicker had been keeping the whole place warm and cozy. And it was silent, as if the church had stopped breathing. From the cross above my head, Jesus just looked at me.

I flew down the steps of the altar and got out of there. But now what? In the hallway I heard whispers. The other kids were there but no one was laughing. Downstairs with the parents and little kids, it took us half an hour to find someone who would give us matches, no questions asked. Then the danged candle wouldn't light and we used up the whole book before we finally got the thing to flicker back to life. It was exhausting, let me tell you. And the guilt! I've never been so relieved to go home.

I had not learned to weigh consequences.

Anyway, when I got married and moved to another city, I didn't feel the need to find another church for almost 15 years.

In the middle of this iffy marriage, though, the need sneaked up on me. By the time Kristal was in eighth grade, I had known for some time that I was unhappy, dissatisfied with my life. Jerry and I owned everything we needed and a whole lot of things we simply wanted—a big house on the water, new cars and a ski boat tied to a buoy out front. We worked hard, but we took lots of three-day weekends and regular trips to Hawaii too.

We were both members of the Chamber of Commerce and active in Gig Harbor's business community. While I ran the Bubblegum Closet, he was busy not only with the tavern, but a movie theater he'd recently opened too. People said they envied us and Kristal's friends teased her that we were rich. We did have material things, but they had no idea what life was really like at our house.

They had no idea that Jerry and I barely spoke. I worked 40-plus hours a week, but was always home for dinner with the kids. He was at work by 6 or 7 A.M. and not home at midnight three or four times a week. I felt like a single parent. Again.

Where was he, all those late nights? Someone—I'd still love to know who—called regularly to tell me. When I'd groggily pick up the phone at 11:30 or so, a voice I couldn't even identify as male or female would whisper to me.

"Jerry is down at Pearl's with Rose," or "Jerry is out back of the tavern, drinking with Sylvia."

What I never figured out is what that person expected me to DO with that information at that hour. Did he want me to drag the kids out of bed and run down there in my jammies with a gun and shoot them both? Was I supposed to leave Kristal and Jeff in their beds and go scream dirty rotten things at him and drag him home? I just didn't have it in me. And if I did shoot him, I just knew I'd end up on the 11 o'clock news in my pajamas. That was the real reason I didn't act. I'd learned a little more about consequences by that stage in my life.

But I kicked myself regularly for getting myself into this mess. If Dr. Phil had been around at the time, I never would have married Jerry. I'd have listened to his advice that "the best predictor of future behavior is past behavior" and walked away.

I knew that infidelity had broken up Jerry's first marriage. To keep his insecurities at bay, however, he needed to maintain a perpetual state of fresh, oh-you're-so-wonderful new love. The kids and I weren't enough to do that for him. After a few years, you're so wonderful just didn't pop up in the conversation much any more.

On alternate weekends, Jerry sometimes took Brian bowling or out in the boat. When he was five or six, Brian casually mentioned the name of some woman who had gone along with them. Somehow I blocked it out. Slowly steamed. Ate when I was angry. I'm ashamed to say that I often yelled at Brian instead of Jerry.

It's a funny thing about infidelity. You don't have to DO something about it until you acknowledge that it's real, that it's happening. It took me years to get to that point. I didn't want to give up on the dream that Jerry would eventually think of someone besides himself.

But I was lonely. I didn't feel married or supported or cherished. I was mad. And this has always confused me—like many women, rather than blaming my cheating husband, I blamed the women in his life. Why do we do that to each other? Anyway, I mouthed off and took potshots at "his barmaids," which once made him so mad that he left for two days without a word. I have always been really good at pushing buttons—you know—the ones below the belt that really inflict pain. I didn't make life easy for him, I'm sure. His own lack of confidence kept him at bay. My mouth drove him off even further.

Around this time, I hired a woman named Sharon to help at the store. She was a nice, competent woman, but seemed a bit strange too. As she vacuumed the floor in the morning, she sang songs to God! She kept switching the radio to a Christian station. If I told her we'd had a great week at the store she said, "Praise the Lord!"

I've worked my butt off! I thought (though I was too polite to yell it out loud). *What did the Lord have to do with anything? Why is He getting the credit?* I would leave the room shaking my head at her obtuseness.

Sharon was always talking about "the Lord." She called herself a Christian in the same way that most people refer to themselves as a mother or an accountant. She brought her Bible to work and talked about Jesus as if he was a friend of hers rather than a character in some moldy old book. That part intrigued me.

I had always considered myself a Christian—I'd spent all those years at Bethlehem Lutheran, after all. I'd even taught Sunday school, for heaven's sake! Unfortunately, my mom yelled all the way home from church every week, which obliterated everything I'd just heard about the love of God.

A few other friends called themselves Christians too. I took aerobics classes from an exuberant, on-fire woman named Jeani. She and her husband Bob were some of the nicest, happiest people I'd ever met. I watched them care for and care about dozens of people. They talked about Jesus too and definitely had something I didn't understand. I felt like they were wrapped in warm quilts, and I was shivering in the cold.

Then Esther invited me to the Alliance Church on Fox Island. She said I needed to come "just to hear the music" because the new pastor and his wife, Andy and Margie, both had beautiful voices. Kristal had been asking me why we didn't go to church, so one day I plucked up my courage and my kids and went.

I'll be dipped if these people didn't have it too! The moment I slipped into a church pew I could just tell. It was weird. A few of them actually scared me by being just too danged friendly. One former missionary even called me at home after church and talked about the Lord for half an hour!

I was wary. But I continued to watch these people, sort of suspiciously, for about a year. I paid attention to what they did, how they lived. It was as if I was waiting for them to screw up—to fall on their faces, to blow up in the face of difficulty, to be mean and nasty or phony, to scream at me all the way home like my mom had. But it didn't happen. Sharon, Bob and Jeani, the people at church—they all seemed genuine and happy.

I still didn't really know what to call it, but I did know that these people had something I didn't. I knew I needed it too.

I was lonely. Married, yes. Kids, yes. Yet I felt like no one cared about me except these friends. They didn't ask about the weather or business. They asked about me, my life, my family. And I finally had to be honest.

I finally admitted to myself that my life was a mess. Once I said the words out loud, the loneliness, the infidelity, the betrayal, the hurt and the pain came pouring out of the bottle, and I knew I'd never be able to shove it all back in again.

After about a year of being in church every week, I went to a concert. Rejoice, a local choir, was performing at what I now considered to be my church. Throughout their performance, I couldn't take my eyes off of Leslie, an alto in the front row. Her face positively glowed. She sang as if she was singing to her bridegroom. The woman was definitely in love with this Jesus she was singing about. She looked like an angel. More than I've ever wanted anything, I wanted to feel like that too.

At the end of the concert, the choir director asked if anyone wanted to "accept Jesus into your heart." I'd heard that line before but had never known what it meant. This time I understood. Leslie had Jesus in her heart. That's why she glowed. He asked us to come to the altar. Yikes! As much as I wanted to, I couldn't make myself walk down there in front of all those people. Instead, I went home alone, thinking about it all the way.

In my bedroom that night, I got down on my knees and talked to God.

"I want to feel the way Leslie feels," I said. "Don't get me wrong, I don't want to LOOK like that, because then everyone will know. But I want the peace she has—the peace that fills her soul so full that it spills out onto her face—the peace that Sharon and Bob and Jeani and all those other people have. I want to be in love with Jesus, too."

I didn't really feel any different when I got up, but somehow I knew God had heard me. I didn't tell a soul about my decision. Over the next several weeks, I did what all good Christians do. I read my Bible. I prayed. I went to church. But I didn't FEEL any different. Didn't feel that peace like I sensed my friends did. One night I talked to the Lord about it.

"I want to FEEL differently," I complained.

And for the first time in my life, I heard God answer me. It wasn't some voice from the clouds. Nothing loud or scary. It just popped into my thoughts as naturally as you please. I knew immediately that it was God.

"If you really want to feel differently," He said, "go get baptized."

Gulp.

That would require going public. I'd have to ask the Pastor about it. He would know. So would my friends. But as I mulled over the prospect, I suddenly wasn't afraid. In fact, I could hardly wait.

The next day I climbed into my blue Bubblegum van and drove to the church to tell Pastor Andy I wanted to be baptized. He didn't lecture or preach, but just smiled and said he'd make the arrangements. Funny, as soon as I told him, I just knew it was right and a peace seemed to fill me. I DID feel different.

By the time I had told Sharon and Bob and Jeani, I knew I was wrapped in that warm comforter of God's. I knew I felt different but I got a little freaked when people began telling me I looked different too. I finally understood the term "peace of the Lord."

Now, about baptism. I believe in the dunking method. I'd read the part in the Bible about Jesus being baptized in the river. Being submerged under the water, then rising up out of it, was supposed to signify rebirth. Since I was really feeling like a new person these days that seemed right. I never did figure out who came up with the sprinkle method, but to each his own.

One of the things I habitually said when I was surprised or newly informed about something was, "Well, I'll be dipped!" One day when this phrase popped out, Kristal said, "Yeah, you WILL be dipped, won't you?" She'd been going to church with me, learning about baptism and the rest of it right beside me. She'd joined the youth group so she understood and shared my faith.

So when planning what non-see-through thing I would wear for this public dunking, I found a gray sweatshirt. But never being one to leave things alone, I got out my fabric paints. I drew a big cross, then wrote "I'll be dipped" in big purple and turquoise letters on the front. I was happy about the prospect of being baptized and thought it might as well show.

I had told Jerry all about my budding faith—in small increments, at least. He couldn't take much at one sitting. I told him how important this was to me and asked him to attend my baptism, where I knew I had to tell people why I wanted to do this and what the Lord meant to me.

I so wanted him to understand. This new thing I had found, this faith in God, had somehow changed me. My heart was lighter. For perhaps the first time in my life I felt safe, cared for, protected, treasured. I don't know how I knew, but I knew, deep in my soul, that God cared about me. When I read Psalm 139 about how He had created me, I knew it was true. That He loved me beyond measure. I could actually feel His love, although I often had trouble believing it could be as easy as asking.

To those who don't get it—heck, I had missed it for 35 years myself—it seems phony, but this new faith of mine was like an enormous gift and I wanted to give it to Jerry. (And my mother and my siblings and the rest of the world too.)

But on that Sunday afternoon when I was dunked in a backyard pool and came out a whole new person, Jerry wasn't there. I don't remember if he was mowing the lawn or napping.

What surprised me most about this new faith was that I couldn't seem to stop crying. I'd always sort of prided myself on being tough, on being able to take whatever was thrown my way without tears (well, except *Little House on the Prairie* episodes and *Hallmark* commercials), but that went right out the window when God got hold of me.

I never made it through a worship service, a Bible study or even a little bitty prayer without tears. Not the sobbing, shaking kind. It was more of a slow leak. I was just so grateful to have found God. It seemed like I'd uncovered an enormous secret. Years of pain seemed to be flowing right out of me. For the next two years, the love of God trickled, quite literally, out of my eyes every time I entered His warm, fully comforter-equipped, presence. I've been knocked flat a few times, but never been truly cold or lonely, since.

4
LIVING A LIE

It wasn't until I met the Lord that I looked my life in the eye. I realized I'd been living a lie. Divorce seemed increasingly inevitable. I hardly saw Jerry any more. When we camped together, he wouldn't watch the sunset until his wheels were polished, so even when he was present, it seemed like he wasn't. Since he always emptied his pants pockets on top of the dryer when he walked in the back door, I sometimes had to look there to see if he was home. I'd been ignoring this situation for years, thinking, unconsciously of course, that if I didn't admit the problem, it didn't exist.

When I finally faced the situation, I asked Jerry to move out. AIDS had just made its debut, and I didn't feel safe sleeping with him any more.

"If you aren't happy with the way things are, you move!"

"What about the kids?" I countered. "Are you going to take care of them?"

In the end, Jerry moved out of the bedroom, but only made it as far as the rec room. He camped down there, coming and going from his dates. One gorgeous summer Sunday, the kids and I were surprised when he showed up shortly after we got home from church. He walked down to the water, where the tide was out and kept looking at our boat, which leaned seriously to the side in only a foot or two of water. The poor thing looked like a beached whale. He kept pacing and running his hands through his dark, curly hair. When he came back in and wandered into the kitchen, I finally asked what was up.

"Well, I was supposed to pick someone up in Tacoma. At the marina," he said.

"Ahhhh," I said, understanding his dilemma and just barely resisting the urge to laugh out loud. "But the tide is out. Bummer. Can you call her?"

"No. I'm late. I'm sure she's already waiting at the dock and the marina isn't open so I can't get hold of her."

I chuckled all afternoon at the thought of her standing there on the dock, waiting, expecting my husband to show up in our boat to show her a good time.

But after about a month of this insanity of Jerry living in the rec room, God began tapping me on the shoulder. That conscience sort of voice whispered in my ear again and I knew I needed to at least attempt to save the marriage. I came up with a plan. One night I cranked up my courage, combed my hair, put on a fresh shirt and went downstairs.

"I'd like to talk to you. To apologize," I began.

"Yeah, I'm listening," he said, barely looking up.

"I'm really sorry that our marriage has turned out this way. I had such high hopes for us. I've been wrong about some things. Made a lot of mistakes. I shouldn't have been disrespectful and sarcastic. I should have included you in the decision-making—like consulting you before I sold my car and bought the Bubblegum van."

"That's true," he said. "You should have told me about that."

"I should have. Please forgive me."

I mentioned a few other specifics like calling his employees barmaids and smacking him on the shoulder with my camera the day he yelled at Kristal. But it seemed that for every specific thing I apologized for, he thought of something I hadn't mentioned.

"Yeah, well, what about . . .?" he kept saying, a little

louder each time.

This was not exactly going as I'd hoped. I thought he might finally admit that he was indeed having an affair with Rose, his business associate/barmaid. Thought he might think of something he needed to apologize to me for. Nope. The old me would have stomped up the stairs at least three times during the course of this conversation, but I didn't scream, didn't smack him upside the head. With God's help and a few deep breaths, I kept my cool. I hadn't yet presented my plan.

"It doesn't seem like either of us has put much effort into this marriage for a long time," I said, delivering my practiced speech. "I won't feel right walking away from it without doing that. I feel like we need to give it one last chance. Then, if it doesn't work, at least I'll know I gave it my all. So, I'd like to propose an idea.

"If I promise to check in with you regularly and be as sweet and kind as I can possibly be, are you willing to try it for 90 days? I can't do this alone. A marriage can't be one-sided. If it's ever going to work, we both need to give it our all. Ninety days is what I'm asking. Can you give up Rose? Can you come home at night in order to be a family? Are we worth 90 days? Are you willing to try?"

I was rambling. Hoping he would respond. He just cocked his head and looked at me as if he was trying to figure out what I was up to. He said he'd think about it. I tromped upstairs not knowing what to think.

"Okay, I'll try it for 90 days," he said before work the next morning.

"Are you sure? Think we can do this?"

"I don't know," he said honestly. "I'll try." Carefully, I pushed one more time.

"So, will you tell Rose it's over today?"

He hesitated and I could almost see our family teeter-tottering in the balance.

"Okay," he said finally, looking aside rather than into my eyes.

For two days he came home at a reasonable hour, tossing his wallet and keys and change on the dryer as usual, the spot I often found things he "accidentally" left there. He ate dinner with us. Played games or watched a movie at night, helped put Jeff to bed. Slept upstairs in the big bed.

The third evening he came home very quietly and immediately went to the garage. On the dryer beside his wallet, I found a loosely-folded, pages-long note in Rose's impeccable handwriting. Of course, I read it. This woman who he had repeatedly claimed not to be involved with claimed to love him more than I did. Said she was better for him than I was, appreciated him more. She loved his boys and could help him reach his potential. She was divorcing her husband to be with him.

There was no point in arguing the matter. The man had staggered and fallen three days into the battle. And, he'd saved himself the chore of telling me by leaving the letter for me to find. Was this the man I wanted in my life?

So, when he walked in the door a little later, I simply held up the letter and shook my head.

"I give up," I said sadly. "At least I can walk away knowing I tried."

I don't recall that he said anything at all. He moved out the next day. Said he was going to live above the tavern, although it was a horrible little attic room I knew he'd never live in. If I needed to speak to him, I could always find him at Rose's.

In my mind, we were divorced that day.

Except for the fact that dinners became more casual, things didn't change much after Jerry was gone. Kristal and Jeff often hung out in the kitchen and helped me cook. We danced around while chopping veggies and cooking delectable meals. Jeff usually sat on the countertop, sniffing the spices and making suggestions on what to add to the soup.

On weekend nights, we sometimes layered tortilla chips, shredded cheddar, black olives, chopped tomatoes, black beans, taco meat and lots of salsa onto a big plate. Hey, nachos contain some important food groups and they taste great!

Kristal and Jeff prepared the pillows on the living room floor and put the movie into the VCR while the nachos were in the oven. Then, when the cheese was all gooey and hot, we laid around the serving plate like the spokes of a wagon wheel while we ate dinner and watched a movie.

Because I always hated making beds alone, we played parachute with the sheets whenever we changed them. When Kristal was little, I'd whip the sheet high into the air and while it was at its peak, she'd jump in the middle, collapsing the parachute. Now, Kristal tossed Jeff into the middle, and we laughed until we collapsed on the bed.

Kristal passed on to Jeff advice on everything from food to fashion. A great Mexican restaurant had opened beside my store and the kids loved their Super Burrito Manderos. Even though Jeff was only five, he was determined to eat the hottest salsa available. An early attempt to be manly, I suspect. Kristal taught him to eat it by avoiding the sensitive tip of his tongue. I thought he might choke as he shoved chips full of it down his throat. To this day, if he has to take any kind of pill, he washes it down with a spoonful of Reser's salsa.

One day I bought Jeff a pair of red OshKosh canvas pants and a striped t-shirt. He tried the outfit on and seemed fine with it—until he ran into the living room to show Kristal. Ever so discreetly, she gave him a look. Didn't say a word. Didn't have to. They spoke the language of the rolled eyes.

"Take this off!" he said immediately, stripping off the shirt and running to his room. He trusted her to help him lead every aspect of his little life.

Kristal could get Jeff to do all kinds of things he'd never do for me. He'd argue if I asked him to pick up his toys, but Kristal made a game out of everything. She'd challenge him to a game of *Beat the Clock* to see who could pick up toys fastest. She could do in two minutes flat what it would have taken several maids to accomplish.

Once at my mother's house, when my hairdresser sister was lining up the family for haircuts, I told Jeff to get ready because he was next. With a shriek, he ran to hide in the bedroom. Kristal didn't say a word. Instead, she quietly found a piece of paper, wrote the number "3" on it, went in and handed it to him.

"When your number is called," she told him in an official-sounding voice, "it'll be your turn for a haircut." His face lit up, and he said, "Okay."

I just stood back and shook my head. The girl was brilliant when it came to handling kids. She absolutely loved being surrounded by children—probably because she'd been the only child and grandchild on both sides of the family for so many years. For whatever reason, Kristal was a natural teacher, but what she wanted more than anything was to be a mother. She wanted a houseful of kids.

Another thing we did once Jerry was gone was get the dog we'd wanted for a while. We found our perfect puppy through the classifieds. He was cute, blond and soft as a whisper. We all had different reasons for choosing Luke. Kristal was too old to dress him in doll clothes like she'd done with our last dog, but she gushed, "He's sooo soft. Just feel this velvety ear." Jeff thought his enormous feet would give him "great traction on a trail." Me? I liked the security of having a good-sized dog around.

We could see that Luke's mother was a Brittany Spaniel. Her owners claimed the father was a marauding black lab. But there was no doubt in my mind that Luke was directly descended from Old Yeller. He had the same build and coloring, the same innocent head tilt. Same goofy smile. Same bent for trouble.

Trouble I didn't need more of. I was just trying to grow two kids into half-way normal adults and pay the bills at the house and at my small store. Luke took our minds off of all of that, which was just what I'd hoped.

While he was teething, Luke chewed up one of my good shoes. I was so mad that I whacked him with it, which guaranteed that he wouldn't touch THAT shoe again. The next day he chose a different pair. I must have tossed at least a dozen pairs before I learned to close my bedroom door.

The first time Luke got too close to our 14-year-old long-haired white cat, Max, I wasn't home. Kristal called me at work to tell me that Max had swatted Luke on the ear.

"It's bleeding all over!" she cried. "Splattering every time he shakes his head. What do I DO?"

She'd tried applying pressure but Luke wouldn't hold still. Jeff was afraid Luke was going to bleed to death. I rushed home and called the vet. He said the cat must have sliced the blood vessel that runs around the edge of a dog's ears and recommended trying to clot the blood with flour. He suggested laying one ear over the top of the other and tying them above his head. *Yeah, right,* I thought, knowing Luke would rip it right off. For future reference—forget wrapping Scotch tape around a wiggly head; wide packing tape is easier to apply, but easy for big paws to remove. Medical tape lasts through two or three vigorous head shakes. Duct tape takes the hair right off with it, which has gotta smart.

Whatever we tried, Luke wouldn't stop shaking his head. Every time, things broke loose again. The kitchen walls and floor looked like a murder scene but we gave up cleaning up the blood spatters. I finally put Luke in his doghouse and left him outside. By the next day, he was just fine.

Kristal babied him. She and Luke would get comfortable on the living room carpet and she'd stroke his big, thick skull and rub his belly while she told him about her latest crush or the fight she'd had with her best friend. It seemed like he understood every word of her sophomore angst.

As he grew to be a linebacker of a dog, Luke became the perfect companion for little boy adventures too. He followed Jeff and his best friend Mike as they built forts and tromped through the overgrown lot between their houses.

One day while doing dishes, I heard a crashing sound in the woods. I flew out the door to find twigs snapping and foliage flying. Jeff stood on one side of the vacant lot beside our house; Mike on the other, near his house. They'd been taking turns calling Luke back and forth.

My young engineer had tied a big blue plastic 55-gallon drum behind Luke so he would forge a trail for them. Brilliant! Jeff had been right about those big paws! Luke plopped down at my feet with the biggest grin on his face—as if he knew he'd done a good job.

Luke and I bonded too, but not until he was housebroken and quit chewing my shoes.

5
LEUKEMIA HITS

We thought our lives were cooking along pretty well when leukemia hit. Kristal was a sophomore, Jeff in kindergarten. I'd just survived the busy back-to-school season at the store, and I had settled into a regular schedule.

None of us were prepared for Kristal's diagnosis, but in the space of one afternoon, we were suddenly fenced in by white, sterile walls. Nurses assigned us to room 301, at the end of the hall "where it will be quiet and private" so we could adjust to life in the hospital.

We got a quick course in Leukemia 101.

"Leukemia is cancer of the blood," we heard (and I'm paraphrasing here.) "Think of the cancer cells as Jack, the big, mean, bully in the neighborhood. Jack chases the red and white blood cells into the alley and pins them down. He hogs all the nutrients for himself. He reproduces over and over to make more of his little mean buddies who beat up on the other guys too. The chemo kills the fastest growing cells in the body—the cancer cells, plus the hair cells and the ones that line the digestive system, which explains baldness, mouth sores and nausea.

"Pretty soon the white blood cells are so weak and puny that they can no longer protect the body, can't fight against infection. Even a common cold can lead to death. The red cells, who are supposed to fill us with vim and vigor, can't. Patients get weaker and weaker. Soon they can't walk, can't stay awake."

Yikes. We were overwhelmed.

So, as soon as Kristal was comfortable in her first-ever hospital room, I made three phone calls. The first was to the prayer chain so they could get our entire church praying. One was to ask Laurie, the friend who was watching Jeff, if he could spend the night at her house.

The last phone call was the one I most needed to, and most hated, to make. I had to check with Jerry about our insurance. Months before we separated, he began to balk about paying for Kristal's health insurance. Thought her own father should pay for it. So, I had checked with Gary, asking him to add Kristal to his policy while Jerry called our insurance company to remove her from our policy. That was months ago and the subject had never come up again.

Now, panic struck in the depths of my heart. Was Kristal covered? After someone wrote leukemia on her chart, I knew I'd never be able to add her to anyone's policy. Had Gary gotten around to adding Kristal to his policy? I wasn't sure.

If the doctors were right about this leukemia, we were in this for the long haul. Cancer can steal years of people's lives. One kind can be cured and another kind can pop up somewhere else. It sometimes costs people not only years of their lives but their houses too. Many times the Bubblegum Closet had helped families on the verge of bankruptcy because of medical bills. This was a huge deal. It could mean the difference between having a home to go home to. I had visions of homelessness. Where would the kids and I go? What would we do if Kristal wasn't insured?

Jerry was shocked to hear about Kristal's diagnosis, of course, but agreed to call the insurance company in the morning. It was going to be a long night.

Nurses brought Kristal her first plate of tepid hospital food. She settled in, meeting a white-haired woman named Joan, who had the biggest, most genuine smile I think I'd ever seen. It was nearly 7 o'clock by now, but Joan said she'd stay with Kristal while I ran home to pack us a few bags. I threw together toothbrushes, clean outfits and jammies for three and dropped off Jeff's bag. By the time I got back to the hospital, I was ready to climb into my little futon on the floor, and Kristal had a best friend named Joan.

Nurses were in and out all night taking temperatures and other things that didn't seem necessary. Kristal and I were both exhausted, but neither of us slept much. So the next morning when Jerry called to say that Kristal was still on our insurance policy, I was stunned. How? I swore that we took her off, I argued. Jerry thought we did too. I was confused but oh-so grateful.

When I mentioned this incident/miracle to the pastor's wife who stopped by, she wasn't even surprised at what I considered to be a write-home-about-it-miracle.

"Sounds like a God thing," Margie said, putting a muffin on a plastic plate for Kristal.

"What?" I said, my mouth hanging open. "What's a God thing?"

"Oh, this kind of thing happens all the time. No one can explain it. But I think that God knows exactly what's going on. I know you're new at following Him, but don't be surprised. He takes care of things—sometimes little things, sometimes huge things like this. We're just going to continue to pray."

And pray I did. I hated being alone in this. Sometimes resented that her dad was not right there beside me. It was exhausting. After that first night, Jeff and I slept on futons on the hospital floor. We'd wake up, rush to get Jeff off to school and me off to work, then rush back to the hospital again. The hospital was about 40 minutes from Fox Island and the running back and forth nearly killed me, but as long as my child was there, I couldn't, wouldn't, leave her alone. She was scared and lonely, and we both relied on God to be there with us until we got the hang of it all.

After school in the afternoon, a carload of Kristal's friends dropped by Kristal's hospital room. Deana, Kerry, Trinna, Kim, Jennifer—they all took turns bringing magazines or books or hanging out to keep Kristal's spirits up. My friends from church or from the store brought dinner or asked Jeff to come home with them after school. Everyone was very helpful and supportive and it seemed no one could believe this was happening to us.

From the first, Dr. Dan and his crew continued to test Kristal's blood. Childhood leukemia is usually Acute Lymphocytic Leukemia or ALL, but they determined that Kristal didn't have that kind. They knew Kristal's condition was acute all right. Turns out that we all run around with those menacing leukemia cells in our blood, but no one gets alarmed until they comprise over 10% of our regular blood cells. It took nearly a week to identify it as Acute Mylocytic Leukemia (AML), which is rare in children because it's the kind old people usually get.

So, Kristal was the exception, not the rule. Surprise, surprise. Dr. Dan said that her chances of survival with Mylocytic were lower than the 90% that's attached to Lymphocytic. *How did we get so lucky to have this harder to cure variety?* I wondered.

The other thing they wanted to do right away was surgery. They wanted to "spare Kristal the trauma of having IV lines in her hands and arms" by installing a Hickman central line. Through this intravenous line, nurses would be able to deliver blood transfusions, chemotherapy drugs or any other medication directly into the vein that led to her heart. It sounded good. For them.

Matter-of-factly, Dr. Dan explained that they would make a two-inch incision in the right side of her chest. They would thread a tube through the vein, leaving about 12 inches of tubing exposed. A flexible, clear material called Tega-derm would then be used to seal the wound and prevent infection. It wouldn't be visible through her clothes. Their final selling point was that she wouldn't constantly be poked by needles because all of her meds could be delivered through the line.

He talked about it like he was talking about having Cornflakes for breakfast in the morning. But this wasn't exactly an everyday event to me. Other than two quick trips to deliver Kristal and Jeff, I'd never been in a hospital. This stuff didn't seem at all normal to me and I just couldn't see it the way they did.

To me, it sounded like they wanted to drug my 15-year-old into unconsciousness. Then, when she was lying there with no wits about her, they'd wheel her into a big sterile room, take a sharp knife and slit open her chest. Cut her wide open! Then they'd stick some sort of clear plastic tube into her vein and ram it straight into her heart. And they were going to leave the tube sticking out! How could a 12-inch tube not be visible?

To top it all off, they wanted me—a person who hadn't even gone through one box of Band-Aids in her entire life— to swab the wound clean and reseal it every day. I thought I had problems with the concept. Kristal hated the idea even more than I did.

Her body was perfect and whole. She didn't have a single scar. No cavities or fillings. Never had a broken bone. I always joked about her sitting in a chair for the first five years, never even getting dirty. Even in preschool, she was not one for mud pies or sand castles. Well, she would have decorated the sand castle, but not built it. She was a girly-girl. When we went to the playground, she'd whiz down the slide and climb the monkey bars, but at home, she played mostly pretend games where she was the teacher, the bride, or the mother. That's what she really wanted.

Now she asked, "How will I ever wear a bathing suit? This thing will be sticking out of me! And can't you just see me at the prom?

"A turtleneck!" she said, with an overdose of sarcasm. "That would be PERFECT—especially if I could find one in black. That's always dressier, isn't it? Maybe I can find one in velour. With sequins!"

We were laughing again, but then she added, "Seriously, Mom, I don't want this stupid Hickman thing. Do I have to?"

She talked to her friend Kerry about it. We went over and over the pros and cons. Not that I allowed her to wear low-cut clothing at 15, but some day she'd want to. Even after it healed, the surgery would leave a permanent two-inch scar in her chest. I didn't blame her for being mad at the thought of a scar where there should be cleavage.

At first, the whole thing had seemed more beneficial to the medical staff than to Kristal. But after days of IV pokes and the constant presence of tubing in her arms, we were both convinced that life would be easier with the Hickman line.

I signed the consent papers—the ones that warn you of all kinds of awful things that can happen under anesthesia. Death and paralysis were right up there on the list. I spent hours trying to find comfort in the hospital's cozy little chapel. I had never had surgery myself and was scared to death for my child.

The next morning in the surgical waiting room, I realized that this was one of the places in the world where no one should be alone. It was worse than being alone at your own birthday party. I continued to worry and pray and wish I were anywhere but there. But in less than an hour, Kristal was out of surgery. Alive. That relaxed me some.

Our down-the-hall neighbor, a 12-year-old named Clayton, who was also from Gig Harbor, had a central line. With serious congenital kidney disease, he'd had kidney transplants and been in and out of the hospital all of his life.

"Piece of cake," he said, waving away our concern. "I've had hundreds of 'em." He and his mom (who I'll call Cindy but I'm not sure that's right) both talked us through this decision and became fast friends in the process. He often tapped on the door to see if Kristal wanted to play checkers or watch a movie.

In the end, the Hickman central line did make life easier for all of us. I became an expert at cleaning it in an ever-expanding circular motion with a Betadine swab. I learned exactly how much Heparin to use to keep the blood in the line from clotting. Kristal never again had to be poked to install IVs.

But one thing still bugs me. Nurses were required to wear gloves just to touch the bottles of chemotherapy drugs, yet they put that poison straight into my baby's heart. It just didn't seem right.

So, after the Hickman, after the diagnosis of AML, chemotherapy began. Each night about 8, a nurse came in and hooked up an IV drip. Of course, we had heard how awful chemo could be. It didn't disappoint. The barfing began immediately.

The idea was to give her the bad stuff overnight so she'd sleep through most of the sickness. Since we were newbies at this, I didn't think to argue the point with them.

Just a few minutes into the chemo protocol, Kristal pulled her emesis basin close. Like it was a teddy bear or something. It seemed to bring her comfort to have it close at hand. In fact, she often had a stack of three or four in case I was emptying one when she needed another. She kept at least one in her hand the entire night. I must have emptied the disgusting thing a dozen times before midnight.

As the evening wore on, there was not much in them. After getting rid of the little bit she'd eaten that day, all that was left was a foul, acrid-smelling clear slime. Kristal hated throwing up. I hated dumping it, but what are you gonna do? Get used to it was pretty much the only choice either of us had.

Doctors had one idea they thought might help.

"There's a drug we can try to keep the nausea under control," Dr. Dan said. "If we give it to you with the chemo, it should help keep your stomach calm."

"Well, it's about time," Kristal said. "What took you so long to tell me about this?"

She signed on immediately. So that night, they gave her Thorazine with her chemo cocktail. Joan brought us a movie and Kristal and I settled in for a peaceful evening.

"I feel awful," Kristal said after an hour or so.

"What do you mean, you feel awful? I thought this stuff was supposed to prevent that. You're not throwing up. What's the problem?"

"I feel like the room is spinning."

"Well, lay down flat. Or try closing your eyes. Maybe that will help."

Nothing helped. In fact, it got worse. Kristal complained of double vision. She felt nauseous. No, she didn't throw up, but the room wouldn't stay in one spot. It kept spinning, but didn't go all the way around. I'd only been drunk three times in my life, but what she described sounded just the same.

We finally talked to Carol, the night nurse, who told us that Thorazine is made from marijuana. Ahhhh, I thought, That explains it. Kristal was just plain mad.

"You mean you're giving me DRUGS?" she said, jerking to an upright position for the first time in hours.

Carol and I cracked up. They'd been giving her drugs every day for a week and this was the first she'd mentioned any objection.

"How can you give me this stuff? Why didn't anyone tell me?" she continued.

She calmed down and closed her eyes. After a few minutes—I think she was praying—Kristal whispered,

"Mom, I've made a decision. If this is what drugs makes you feel like, I swear I will never, ever take drugs. Why would anyone want to feel this awful? My mouth is dry and my brain is fuzzy. I can't think. I feel like I'm out of control. I never want to feel like this again! And I'm not taking this Thorazine stuff again either. I'd rather puke."

As soon as she nodded off, I headed for the chapel, where I thanked God for the lesson Thorazine had taught my daughter.

6
HOSPITAL LIFE

Since we were there for weeks at a time, Mary Bridge Children's Hospital became home to us. Oh, there were horrors—especially for Kristal—but we no longer panicked at the sight of blood. The antiseptic smells came to mean that our friends on the cleaning staff had just been there. We knew those beige barf pans were called emesis basins and that cancer treatments were like recipes doctors called protocols. We pronounced Ara-C and Triptimiacin like pros.

We knew the inside workings—like where they kept the extra blankets, the latest novels and the scrubs. The nurses became good friends. And when they were busy, I often comforted a crying child or a crying mom and went after a Popsicle for one of Kristal's neighbors. Jeff knew where Joan kept the Legos, puzzles and trucks, knew the kid in the next room and which disease he had. While their siblings were getting all the attention, Jeff and Clayton's little brother often raided the toy closet.

Just when we got to feeling sorry for this mess we were in, we'd get someone new next door who was handling WAY more than we were. Like a ten-year-old who had dealt with Cystic Fibrosis every day of her life or a six-year-old brought in with severe head injuries after his father pulled his sled behind the family truck. One day a little girl was brought in with Lupus and I heard her father wailing in the stairwell in the middle of the night. She had died the very night she was admitted. There were a lot of people in the hospital to remind us that we didn't have it so bad, really.

Since Kristal couldn't go to school, the school district assigned her a tutor. She went through a couple of them. They just didn't get the fact that she'd been puking her guts out all night so she couldn't always keep her eyes open during their scheduled appointment. I think they labeled her difficult, but I knew it was the treatments, not Kristal's personality.

One afternoon in Kristal's room, a visitor arrived— Diane, a woman who owned Gig Harbor's quilt shop. I didn't know her well, but whenever I saw her at business association meetings, she was charming and funny. Laughter seemed to follow her. Her shop was located in Gig Harbor's historic Hunt Mansion, a Southern plantation sort of a house with three-story white pillars and an elevator. Wisteria fluttered purple and pretty from the upper balcony, where Diane and her husband lived.

The entire first floor of the house was filled with extravagant, incredible quilts. Although I never bought one, I loved wandering through her shop. But since she had never met Kristal, I was surprised to see her at the hospital.

"You're probably wondering why I'm here," she said, echoing my thoughts exactly. They must be written on my transparent face again.

"I've brought you something," she said, when I introduced her to Kristal. She held out a bulky package. Thrilled, Kristal quickly unwrapped a beautiful, lighter-than-air aqua blue quilt.

"I thought you might put it on your bed while you're here," Diane said. "You know, to make it feel more like home."

Diane explained that the pattern was called Grandma's Garden. Each one of its hundreds of hexagon-shaped calico fabrics had been stitched by hand. In one corner someone named Kathy had embroidered her name and dated it '84. Although I'd never made one, I fully appreciated the months of work that must have gone into this gorgeous old-fashioned quilt.

"This is a little weird, I know," Diane said sheepishly, running her fingers over it, "but I feel like this quilt spoke to me."

"Oh? What'd it say?"

"It said, 'Take me to Kristal.'"

"Hmmm," was all I could think of to say.

"I think I'll name this quilt Mr. Ed," Kristal said suddenly.

"Huh? Why?" Diane and I said in unison.

"Because it spoke to you," she said to Diane with a giggle, wrapping it around her shoulders like a mink.

We all laughed and chatted as we spread the quilt over Kristal's bed. Then a funny thing happened. The room itself seemed to perk up. Perhaps it was the quilt, perhaps the laughter, but the hospital room we had lived in for months suddenly became more familiar, more comfortable.

Mr. Ed became one of Kristal's favorite possessions. Every time she had to return to the hospital, it was the first thing in the suitcase. No matter which room she was assigned (we preferred 301 because it was quieter at the end of the hall), Mr. Ed made it seem remarkably like "home away from home."

To this day, no matter where I am in the world, Mr. Ed will always be within reach. And I'll always wish I could tell Kathy how much I appreciate her work.

One person we could not have survived the hospital without was Joan. Her title was Volunteer Coordinator and yes, she booked the church choirs who sometimes sang in the halls and the devoted ladies who pushed the book cart around once a week, but her job description was much bigger than that. Patient advocate, maybe. Superwoman, even better. Joan had soft white hair, a smile brighter than operating room lights and a laugh she had to throw her hand across so the kids clear down the hall could sleep.

Joan knew what people needed at all times and she could be more than one place at once. She laughed with us and cried with us. She brought in nail polish for Kristal and me and a set of Construx for Jeff. When anything negative happened, she could fix it. Give her a few minutes and she could get her hands on Superman pajamas or a VCR and a movie we'd been waiting to see. The only thing she could never see was someone sneaking a puppy into a kid's room.

Joan and Kristal became fast friends. She and I became fast friends. And every family in every room felt the same way. The woman was amazing. She stayed with Kristal when I went to the courthouse to finalize my divorce. When I returned, freshly divorced and all alone, they made me laugh. When Kristal got depressed because her friends were too busy to visit, Joan and I wrote songs about lipids and chemo and sang them to her. No one in my life has EVER made me do stuff like that—and have fun while I was at it. In the middle of chemo, we laughed. And laughed. And laughed.

We loved the nurses too. Sue was like family. Debbie, Jan and Kathy too. And even if we'd never met most of their families, we knew their stories and what happened to their kids in school the day before.

Strange as it might sound, we had a routine in the hospital and we were comfortable, bordering on happy there. We knew just what to expect. After Kristal finished a round of chemo, she often needed a transfusion to kick-start her energy level. She got packed red cells and platelets, both of which came fresh out of the refrigerator in a bag that nurses hung on her IV pole. Nurses connected the bag into her Hickman line, which ran the platelets straight into her heart. It was routine—except for that one transfusion.

One day Kristal's favorite nurse walked in humming.

Debbie was always in a good mood, kind and young and cute and professional. She hooked up the bag, traded jokes as usual, then was called out of the room. About two minutes later, Kristal pulled Mr. Ed up around her chin.

"I'm cold," she said with a shiver. Within a few minutes, Kristal was shaking. I wondered if she was having some sort of reaction to the blood. Her reaction intensified quickly and she soon looked like she was having some sort of seizure. She curled up in a fetal position with her teeth chattering.

Heck with that lame little buzzer—I stuck my head out the door to yell for help. Debbie came running. Shocked at Kristal's violent shaking and the blue cast to her lips, she quickly assessed the situation and checked the IV.

"Oh, no!" she said, tightening the little plastic wheel on the clear tubing. The bag was nearly empty. I knew immediately what had happened. "I'm SOOO sorry. I left the drip open."

Instead of slowly dripping the big bag of platelets into the IV the way it's properly done, she had left the line wide open, allowing the entire bag of ice cold platelets to run in immediately. The cold had to have chilled Kristal's heart. I had no idea what that could cause, but I was scared to my core.

Debbie ran to get warm blankets and heating pads. I grabbed all the extra sheets and blankets from the cupboard and piled them on top of her. I hopped up on the bed and laid on top of Kristal, willing my body heat into hers, praying for her the whole time. Her teeth chattered so violently that I was afraid she'd bite her tongue. I wrapped myself around her and prayed. She shivered and shook so hard that I had to hang on to the metal rails on the sides of the bed.

Debbie and Joan ran in with a stack of the heated blankets they use in surgery. We tucked them around her and I crawled back in too. Slowly, after about half an hour,

Kristal's shaking slowed. Debbie didn't leave her side, apologizing the entire time.

One friend suggested that I sue them for this mistake. But how could I do that? It was horrible and scary while it lasted, but it was a simple mistake. Debbie meant no harm and she felt terrible about it. We were like family. People don't sue families.

Still, incidents like that shook me. Watching your child so sick, not knowing what is happening or what will happen took a toll on me. I tried not to show fear or exhaustion or total panic around Kristal. Mothers have to be strong for their children, right? If I was afraid, she'd be afraid and I didn't want that.

Sometimes I talked to Joan, who knew exactly what was going on. But other than her, I didn't have anyone to talk to. Yes, I had friends. They sometimes visited for an hour or so, but they didn't live in a small white room like we did. They had no idea how much strength it takes to pretend to be strong. I got so weary.

My safe place, the only place I allowed myself to fall apart, was my car. At least once a week I'd barely make it to my car in the secluded parking lot before wrapping my arms around the steering wheel, putting my head down and sobbing. I could be honest only with God because I knew He wouldn't judge, but just listen patiently.

Once, when I tried to drive home with tears still pouring down my face, I had to slam on my brakes. My body jerked forward so hard that the seat belt grabbed me. I pulled over to the side of the road. Somehow I found it comforting—like that little strap holding me was like God saying, "I've got you. Go ahead and cry."

After that, on the really bad days, I'd jerk forward so that my seat belt would grab me and hold me tight. That little strap felt like the only thing that was keeping me on this earth—like a physical connection to a God without arms. I talked with Him throughout the day. I met Him in the little chapel and in the car. I read His word whenever I could.

I didn't know how it was possible, with Him being in the heavens and me stuck here in a giant mess here on earth, but God had become my best friend.

7

GOODBYE HAIR, HELLO FAMILY

One day we overheard one nurse tell another about someone who couldn't get pregnant because chemotherapy caused her to be sterile. Kristal's face fell. The news hit her like a whip. It devastated her to realize she'd never have babies. As soon as the nurses left, she began to cry.

"Isn't it enough that I have to deal with this stupid leukemia?" she asked through noisy tears. "Even if I live through all of this crap they keep putting into my system—even if the stuff WORKS, I'll never have children! What is the point? How can they give me this poison? Why didn't anyone tell me? Why would God DO this to me? I should never have taken it at all!"

I felt awful. Sterility just hadn't come up and I hadn't been aware of it either. It was probably on the list of side effects—along with nausea, vomiting, possible hair loss and a bunch of other things—but the top three seemed much more immediate, so I guess we just overlooked the fact that she might never have children of her own. Now, she grieved as if she were experiencing a miscarriage.

My heart broke for her. As in too many other instances these days, all I could do was hold her. My beloved child was carrying an unfair load. This was one of the days that it threatened to break her fragile little shoulders. And since longevity does not run in my family, I wondered if I'd be there to hold her when she had to watch all of her friends having babies.

But Kristal never dwelt on her problems. That day, she decided that she'd adopt. But then we had also just met Eddie.

All the nurses had been talking about an adorable almost-three-year-old blond that had been in the Intensive Care Unit for weeks. He had been abused by his mother in California so the state had sent him to live with his father in Tacoma. But his father beat him too, kicking him so hard that his spleen had burst. An operation to repair the damage left Eddie with a thick, sideways scar that ran from the middle of his front to the middle of his back. Because he used his feet instead of his hands to pick up crayons and things, social workers suspected that he'd been tied in his crib for months. Given toys and attention, he quickly learned to use his hands.

Finally, Eddie graduated to the room across the hall from us. He was a charmer, all right. One night, when Kristal was sleeping and the nurses were busy, I heard him crying. I went to his room to pray for and sing to him until he quieted. Within a few days, he allowed me to rock him. With two fingers in his mouth, he'd sometimes reach up to touch my face. Jeff had always wanted a little brother so he played Legos or trucks with Eddie. Funny—Jeff's trucks usually raced and crashed a lot, but when he played with Eddie, Jeff saw to it that the trucks obeyed the rules of the road.

When he had first arrived at the hospital, Eddie didn't speak, but he learned quickly. He knew the nurses by their names, of course. Since my kids called me Mom, that was the only name he had for me. The first time Eddie called me Mom, I could have melted right into the rocking chair. Weeks later, when he was finally well enough to leave his room, Jeff loaded Eddie into a little red wagon and pulled him, with his IV contraption tied on behind with a dish towel, down the hallways. Eddie often joined us for games or movies in

Kristal's room, and we would have adopted him on the spot if he'd been available.

All three of us were heartbroken when the state of California found Eddie and his equally adorable little sister a new home elsewhere. Eddie had helped us too. He had allowed us to take our minds off of ourselves and our own problems for a while. Funny how doing something for someone else often helped me more than it helped them. Although Eddie is a young man by now, I still pray for him.

The down side to spending all of this time at the hospital was that more than once Jeff woke to find that one of his friends had died in the night. My young son came to understand illness and death way too early. I wonder now if I should have protected him more, but perhaps he is better off for knowing life as it truly is—difficult and temporary. And wonderful at the same time.

Kristal fought nausea every day. You'd have thought her emesis basin was a favorite stuffed animal for all the time she spent snuggled up to it on the bed.

It began each day about an hour after her evening dose of Ara-C. Her stomach muscles pulled tight and caused her to retch into the basin again and again, whether she had anything in her stomach or not. Sometimes it didn't stop for six or eight hours. She often didn't sleep until well after midnight.

Her hair didn't fall out right away. We'd heard that it would, of course. My sister had given her a sassy new short haircut—just in case—so that it wouldn't be so traumatic if it happened. But she and I both prayed that she would be the one in a thousand to dodge that bullet. For a while we dared to hope that God had granted our wish.

One morning in the hospital shower, though, as Kristal dried her hair, she pulled the brush away after the first few strokes to find it full of sandy blonde hair. "Aaaauh!" was all I heard before her voice broke.

I rushed in to see what was happening. When I saw the brush, which looked as if it hadn't been cleaned out for months, I knew. She looked at me, big tears rolling down her face. Of all the scary things that cancer meant to her, this had been her biggest fear.

"I just want to be a normal kid," she cried as I crossed the room to hold her. "I wanna blend in, not stand out in a crowd. How many sophomores are BALD? Even the boys all have hair! What am I going to do!?"

She fell into my arms, sobbing. This kid—my child—who rarely cried, was beside herself with grief.

I felt helpless. All I could do was hold her and stroke her back. Mothers, I thought, are supposed to able to fix things—to blow on booboos, put on Band Aids and make the pain go away. How in the world could I make this pain go away?

I couldn't imagine what life would be like without hair, but if I couldn't deal with the thought of it at my age, how in the world would my teenager? How would she handle people's stares? What could I tell her? There were no words.

My identity was pretty attached to my longish blond hair, but I would have chopped it off immediately if it would have helped Kristal. Shoot, it would have saved me at least a half hour of drying and curling every morning, but it just wouldn't have served a purpose. I felt like a failure as a mother.

"Oh Sweetie," I told her. "I'm so sorry. I prayed this wouldn't happen. We'll get some great hats and see what we can do about finding that wig we talked about."

I gently unwound her fingers from the brush and cleaned the hair out of it. As lightly as possible, I finished brushing her hair, but it came out in handfuls and I had to clean it out two more times before I finished. Heartbreaking.

Alas, the wig didn't work. We had it hand-tied, custom-colored in a darling style. I won't admit how much it cost, but trust me, it was a fortune in any single mother's budget. She only wore it twice.

"It itches," she whined. "It hurts my head."

After what I'd spent on it, I felt like strangling her, and told her she'd have to pay me back if it took her ten years. We ended up donating the thing to the children's oncology center, hoping it would go to a child with a less sensitive head.

When Kristal finally returned to school, she did so with her head held high . . . and totally bald. And some funny things happened.

The mother of one of Kristal's friends, for instance, happened to be at school one day. When her daughter got home that afternoon, she told her about the striking student she'd seen there.

"She was gorgeous!" the mother said. "Totally bald with great high cheekbones. She must be a European exchange student or something. Do you know her?"

"Know her?" the girl said with a laugh. "Mom! You know her too! That was Kristal!"

Kristal looked different, all right. All that time she spent with the emesis basin had resulted in the loss of at least 25 pounds. Incredible high cheekbones had appeared out of nowhere and made her eyes look enormous. The singer Shania Twain had shaved her head at about the same time and Kristal looked a lot like her. Classy. Elegant. Strong.

She was strong. The thing was—I had no idea how strong.

After those first weeks of chemo, doctors did another bone marrow test. Dr. Dan announced that Kristal's leukemia was in remission. The cancer was gone! God had answered our prayers! There were no more leukemia cells in her blood.

Ecstatic, we praised the Lord for His mercy and grace. Sure, God had used chemo and doctors, but He's the One who gave them the brains to invent that stuff, right? We were thrilled to be through with this entire nightmare!

"Next, we'll begin another round of chemo," Dr. Dan told us after giving us the good news.

Kristal and I looked at each other, shocked.

"What do you mean?" I asked, confused. "Why? The cancer is gone."

"The normal protocol is two years of further intermittent doses," Dr. Dan said. "It's a preventative measure to make sure the cancer doesn't return."

"Why in the world would I take more chemo?" Kristal asked, getting a little heated. "God has already healed me!"

This was the way they always did it, he said, then went on to the treatment plan he recommended. We listened carefully and finally said we'd discuss it and get back to him.

Kristal and I went home and considered every aspect of the doctor's recommendations. Basically, we argued for a week.

"But the doctors must know what they're doing," I said. "They do this for a living, you know. What if they're right? You could be risking your life by not taking the treatment."

"Look," my totally confident child said, losing patience with me. "God healed me. And if I truly believe that… and I do…then isn't it like a slap in His face to take the chemo? Why would I do that?

"Isn't that saying that I don't believe in Him after all? That I don't believe He healed me? That I don't believe anything else He said?"

I didn't know what was right. In the end, we compromised. We agreed that she would have checkups as often as the doctors advised and that if the tests showed any sign of cancer, she promised to resume chemo immediately.

How did this 15-year-old have more faith than I did? She was somehow filled with the peace of God and it passed my understanding all right. It gave her the strength and confidence to go against her doctor's advice—which is more than I could say.

Me? I watched her like a hawk for any sign of illness.

Some friends applauded our faith; some thought we were insane. Donna, a friend from church, looked at me with enormous eyes when she heard.

"What are you trying to do?" she asked, probably louder than she intended. "Kill her???"

Donna's words sometimes still haunt me.

One Saturday, Kristal, Jeff and I were out running errands. Jeff's hair was a little sloppy so a stop at the barbershop was on the list. Kristal's hair had grown back in and was about an inch or an inch and a half long at the time. She wore it spiked up to make it look a little more stylish.

Kristal and I sat there reading 4-wheeling magazines while Jeff was in the chair. He was getting his usual crew cut because, "I love the way the wind feels on my head when I run." So, with Jeff in his new short cut, we were on the way out the door when a woman stopped us.

"Ohhh, they're like twins!" she exclaimed. "They wear their hair just alike!"

Before her words were carried off in the wind, we all stopped on the sidewalk. At first we just looked at each other in astonishment, but before the next second began, we all cracked up. We doubled over in laughter. The poor woman had no idea how offensive she was—calling a 15-year-old and a 5-year-old twins. A boy and a girl. How dumb. It was hilarious.

"As if I would do this to my hair on purpose!" Kristal said.

"And why would I want to look like my sister?" Jeff spat. "I do NOT look like a girl!"

But that wasn't the end of stupid things people said. At about the same time, Kristal was helping me at the store after school one day. She was still weak and a little wobbly from the months of chemo. When it was time for a break, she grabbed her purse and headed for the Dairy Queen, which was located at the other end of the shopping complex.

"Be back in a sec," she said as she took her skinny self out the door.

A middle-aged customer I didn't know was standing at the counter while I bagged her purchases. She watched Kristal go, shaking her head in what I, at first, didn't recognize as disgust.

"I can't believe teenagers these days," she began, wagging her head as if to scold Kristal. "Why do they DO that to themselves?"

I didn't respond at first. For once I made my words stop for a milli-second before I let them jump out of my mouth. Somehow, I saw my daughter through a stranger's eyes. Kristal did look like an ad for anorexia. Although she didn't wear white makeup and her hair wasn't dyed black, it was spiked up on the top of her head, so I understood why she would think that.

"That girl is my hero," I finally said quietly, not looking up at her. "She has cancer and she fights harder to live than anyone I've ever known. Every day is a struggle for her, and I'm so proud to know her."

The woman didn't say another word. She just lifted her head and walked out the door. I don't remember ever seeing her again.

But her comments made me think. How many times had I judged someone just by looking at them? Those people had stuff going on in their lives that I had no idea about. They didn't deserve to be judged any more than Kristal did. That lady taught me not to jump so quickly to conclusions about people.

8

MERRY CHRISTMAS

It was nearly Christmas. Without Jerry the holidays would be different this year. We wouldn't have to race to see both families on Christmas Eve, but wouldn't see Brian either so the kids and I would miss him. There was no question about going to my parents' house for Christmas dinner. That was always the same.

Before we even got out of the car, we could see it. The candles and the tree glowed through the front windows. Mom's red tablecloth peeked through from under the lace one. The old claw-foot dining table where my dad had had a tonsillectomy when he was four had been extended to seat us all. And in the center, as always at Christmas, sat a poinsettia in the big crystal bowl. The pile of presents spilled out from under the tree. My siblings had all brought their spouses or dates.

For some reason that never made sense to me, South Dakotans eat oyster stew on Christmas Eve. The oysters had to be imported from half a continent away, but hey, it was tradition. We rushed through our oyster stew and deli sandwiches, but couldn't dive into that pile of gifts until the dishes were finished and the kitchen sparkled. Only then did we gather around the fireplace.

Before we opened gifts or attended candlelight services at church, Dad settled into his favorite chair and opened the big fat family Bible. December 24 was a big day for that Bible. Although it lived permanently on the coffee table, this was the only time the poor cover was opened all year. Dad found the bookmark in Luke 2 and started reading the Christmas story.

"In those days Caesar Augustus issued a decree…"

I loved this part. We sat there hushed in the candlelight, listening. I don't recall a single time my mother ever read me a story, but this was Dad's night. It was the one time all year my siblings sat quietly and listened to God's word. It was peaceful. Quiet. Reverent. A great tradition.

But I did wonder how my life might have been different if we'd read that Bible a little more often. How can anyone know who God is unless they read His word? My siblings laughed at my relationship with the Lord. I knew they weren't ready to hear my opinion on the subject, so I knew better than to bring it up.

Anyway, when my parents later announced that they were retiring to Arizona, the first thought that popped into my head was, "Who's going to read the Christmas story?"

Usually, my family was not quite so reserved. Until Jeff came along, Kristal was the only grandchild in the family. So, when my sisters and older brother gathered for birthdays or holidays at Mom's, Kristal had always gotten a lot of attention.

She often helped Grandma serve dinner or dessert. When she was four or five, my mom had made her a little white apron and she began to curtsy as she delivered pie to those sprawled in the living room after dinner. My Dad tipped her when she brought his favorite pumpkin pie and her pockets were soon jingling with change.

We all thought it was cute when this kindergartner decided she wanted to be a waitress when she grew up. Grandma gave her a little pad of paper and she began taking orders for the kind of pie everyone wanted. Cute.

But it didn't last. My family decided she needed a reality check.

"Apple pie with ice cream," my 6'4", 300-pound brother said. But when she delivered it with a curtsey, he boomed, "Wait a minute. This isn't what I wanted. This pie is cold. No one eats apple pie cold."

"Oh, I am sooo sorry," she said apologetically, grabbing the pie to return it to the kitchen so grandma could heat it up. My sister picked up the game.

"Hey, waitress, this fork has a spot on it. Would you mind bringing me a clean one?"

We chuckled. Kristal took the first couple of complaints like a pro. Cold coffee? I'll get you a fresh cup. What? Not enough whipped cream? One moment, please. I'll get some more. She was running back and forth to the kitchen to fix whatever problem my siblings came up with. We were cracking up.

But gang mentality kicked in. Within three minutes, things got ugly. Our complaints got louder and meaner and probably closer to what real waitresses face every day. Every time the poor kid turned her back, we quaked with muffled laughter.

Finally, Kristal started to get a little huffy. "That's exactly what you ordered, Ma'am," she told me with attitude.

When my brother shoved a piece of pie at her and bellowed in his enormous voice about it being the wrong kind, she shoved back. "Well, if you don't like it," she finally said with her hands on her little hips, "you can just find yourself another restaurant!"

"That'll teach you to be a waitress," he said, grabbing her around the waist and tickling her. "At least you know what you're getting into."

That was the last time she told anyone in my family she wanted to be a waitress. It was a great game—and typical of how we learned anything at my house. Humor and humiliation always went hand in hand. But none of us knew how that lesson in standing her ground would serve her later in life.

Like this year. Kristal had fought hard and was now in remission. She was getting stronger every day. Her hair was coming back in—even if it was closer to brown than blond this time. All was well. This leukemia deal was over. We were praising God. Well, Kristal, Jeff and I were praising God. The rest of my family thought we were a little weird because they never did that themselves. Mom and Dad called themselves Christians, just like I used to, but they had no idea how much more God had to offer them.

In January, Kristal went back to school. Once a month, she and I went to the clinic at Mary Bridge for blood tests. When it was over, we'd cross the street to Frisko Freeze, Tacoma's famous old-time eatery, for a greasy burger or an ice cream cone. With juice from our burgers dripping down our arms, we laughed all the way home.

Because we were so grateful to God, we attended church and Bible studies even more diligently. We thanked Him regularly for the miracle He had done. Through this difficult year, I had always taken time to attend Bible Study Fellowship every week. I had learned so much and loved getting to know all the terrific women in my small group. Our knowledge and trust in the Lord was growing week by week. Kristal added the youth group to her schedule and began hanging out with kids from church.

As tough as Kristal was, she still struggled with peer pressure. Missing months of school hadn't helped and she really missed hanging out with her friends. Just like any other sophomore, she wanted to fit in. She'd once been voted funniest girl in class and even her kindergarten teacher had classified her as a social butterfly, not a scholar.

Now, I know it may sound like I'm one of those mothers who believes her child is perfect. Huh-uh. I have proof to the contrary. Yeah, she screwed up along the way, just like every other kid. Kristal always had trouble getting going in the morning. On occasion, she missed the bus, and I had to drive her to school. Let me just say that I've never fully appreciated surprises, especially when they disrupt my busy morning. Even though we lived on an island, I could handle it when I had to drive right by her elementary school on my way to work.

But by the time Kristal was in middle school, we were in a whole new ballpark. And it didn't help that middle school starts an hour earlier than elementary school. The school district must have gotten a good price on this land. They built the middle school on a piece of property 20 minutes from nowhere, which meant a 40-minute roundtrip for me. That put me WAY late every time she missed the stinkin' bus. I was not a happy camper and tended to lecture her on responsibility the entire way, which didn't make her a happy camper either.

I was always a tough mom. I cracked down. I believe kids learn through natural consequences of their actions—you write on the wall, you wash it off—that sort of thing. But when a taxi service opened in Gig Harbor, I had a brilliant idea for a natural consequence to habitual tardiness.

I made Kristal call to find out how much it would cost for the taxi to pick her up on Fox Island and take her to Kopachuck Middle School. I think they quoted $12. I told Kristal I'd do it for half of that, but that I was going to start charging her every time she missed the bus. When it cost her several hours of babysitting money, she hustled a bit more in the morning. I think she only paid me twice. Problem solved.

But compared to leukemia, tardiness was a very small problem.

"I just want to be normal," she had said over and over during her illness.

On the up side, all this time we'd spent together had given us time to talk about the things "normal" kids sometimes get into—drugs, booze, sex. I tried to teach her to spot the dangers that lurk in the dark. She loved hearing stories of my old mistakes and, since they might help her avoid the same stupidity, I didn't mind telling her about my foibles.

She knew about the homecoming game right after my graduation when Judy Otani puked all over my dad's car and I had to dig peas and carrots out of the bib and tuck upholstery. She knew I had been too shy to say a word while my ninth grade boyfriend sped through neighborhood streets at 95 miles an hour. She knew I had nearly crashed my mother's big Olds 98 when I drove it 110 mph on the freeway. And she knew my morals had caved when I was engaged to her father, and that I was pregnant when I married him.

We made a deal. Kristal had always been a good kid, but I told her that if she ever got into trouble, she could call me to pick her up, no questions asked. But I didn't expect the call to come from a party with the church youth group.

It was the first barbeque of the season and Kristal rode with friends to a house just up the hill. She had attended many of these events in the past so I knew just what to expect—about 30-40 teens, all toting chips, snacks or soda, depending on whether their last names began with A-F, G-N or O-Z. We Walstons always brought the drinks, it seemed. But someone else had brought drinks to this party as well—apparently under a big beach towel.

Anyway, Jeff was in bed and I was minding my own business about 10 o'clock that night when Kristal called. Whispering.

"Mom?"

"Huh?" I could barely hear her.

"I need you to come get me," she said "Now. And yell at me."

"Okay. Be right there."

I drove down the tree-lined drive to a fabulous house that lay hidden in the woods. In the yard, I saw a few kids I recognized, but Kristal wasn't with them.

"Where's Kristal?" I barked out the driver's side window.

"I'll find her," one volunteered as they all scurried away. I climbed out and stood against the fender with my arms crossed.

Within one minute, she arrived. "What?" she asked, arms outstretched.

"You were supposed to be home by 10, remember?" I said in my mean voice.

"But…"

"Don't even start," I said, pointing. "Just get in the car!"

She rolled her eyes and made one of those exasperated noises that teenagers are so good at, then yanked open the car door and plopped into the seat. Before we even made it back to the road, she let out an enormous breath.

"Thanks," she said, leaning her head against the seat.

"Was I mean enough?" I asked with a laugh.

"Yeah, perfect," she said. "A couple of new guys brought beer and some other booze. I hate beer and didn't want to try the other stuff but I was running out of excuses. I didn't know how to get out of it."

"I'm proud of you, Kiddo," I said, poking her playfully with my elbow.

We giggled, feeling conspiratorial. When we pulled onto the road, I hit the gas and we laughed like Bonnie and Clyde escaping a bank robbery. Our plan had worked, and I didn't care if her friends thought I was a mean mother. Kristal was safe. I admired her for being far more gutsy than I had been at her age.

A year or so earlier, when she should have spoken up, she hadn't. One Friday night when she was in 9th grade, Kristal had invited two new friends over to spend the night. I'd met these girls and their parents a couple of times over the years, but didn't know them well. Let's call them Thelma and Louise.

The three of them watched a movie with Jeff and me in

the living room, then tromped downstairs to Kristal's room. I heard them giggling for a while, then things got quiet so I assumed they had gone to bed. Naïve, very naive.

When Jerry got home and crawled into bed around 11 that dark, rainy night, he asked if Kristal was home.

"Sure," I said like the trusting mother I was, confident in my daughter's character. "She has friends spending the night. Why?"

"Well, when I turned off the bridge, I saw three girls huddled under an umbrella. I didn't see their faces, but they seemed young to be out so late."

"Well, it couldn't be her. She'd never do anything like that," I said, rolling over.

But I couldn't sleep. What if it was Kristal? Na. Go to sleep. But after about five minutes of turmoil, I threw back my nice, warm quilt and trudged downstairs to check. They weren't playing pool or the jukebox in the family room. Kristal's room was empty and they weren't in the bathroom either. Aaauugh!

Panic rushed into my gut with the force of a freight train. Where could they be? Why would they leave? Kristal had never sneaked out of the house before. Who WERE these little hooligans that I had allowed in my house? And where had they taken my daughter? We lived on a rural island with quiet lanes and no streetlights. They wouldn't have crossed the bridge. Would they? Where could they have gone?

I threw on some jeans and a sweatshirt and ran to the car. Jerry slept peacefully. I drove carefully through the stormy night, peering down every driveway. Nothing. I drove to the bridge and back again. Maybe they went to Kristal's friend, Kim's, I thought. She lived only a few blocks away. But Kim's house was totally dark and I couldn't very well pound on the door and wake them up.

The girls must be back by now, I thought, turning back down my own street. Nope. They hadn't come back. I paced.

I prayed. I went out looking again, this time all the way to the Deanna's at the other end of the island. Nothing. When I got back again, they were STILL not home. I paced like a mother bear.

By now it was after midnight. I went to the phone book and called Thelma's parents, whom I had met a few times. I had visions of them suing me for losing their child. Murder and mayhem. Headlines like: Three teens found dead in ditch—things like that twitched through my mind.

"Ummm…" I started when the dad answered sleepily. "I'm sorry to call so late but this is Shirley Walston and your daughter is spending the night with my daughter, Kristal. But I just discovered that they're not here. She's never done anything like this before. Do you have any idea where they might have gone? Does Thelma have a boyfriend on Fox Island? Could they be there?"

"Not that I know of," he said. "I wouldn't worry about it. Thelma's done this before."

Aauuughh!

"What do you MEAN she's done this before?" I wanted to scream. But even at that hour, in that situation, I didn't want to offend him.

"Where did she go that time?" I said instead. "Do you know of anyone they might have visited? They don't even have driver's licenses. Who might have picked them up?"

"No, I don't know," he said sleepily. "If they don't get back by morning, just give us a call."

Or perhaps he didn't say that part until the second time I called. Whatever. I thought my mind would explode! How could parents be so casual when their young girls are out in the night? Alone. I was frantic with worry. I got out my Bible and tried to concentrate. It didn't work. I cried. I paced. I got in the car and drove around again.

Finally, at nearly 1 in the morning, I decided to call Louise's mother whom I'd met only once.

"I'll be right there," she said immediately.

Finally! Some action here! I liked this woman! I thanked God that I was not in this alone any longer. I sent up a few prayers of appreciation, and with ten minutes several things happened at once. First, I heard a noise and ran to the stairs. Kristal sheepishly met me there, drying her dripping head with a towel. But before we could speak, a car pulled down the driveway, and we went to the front door. Thelma and Louise slipped out of the car and came in. I was not gracious, not really thinking about hospitality at that point.

"Get out of my house," I snarled with my arms crossed. "Go get your stuff and get out of here."

Heads down, they scooted downstairs. Helen, the mom, apologized, of all things, and said that this would not happen again. She had picked up Thelma and Louise on the road. She and the girls left within two minutes of their arrival.

"I am so sorry," Kristal said, breaking into tears and falling into my arms when we were finally alone. "I was sooo scared."

Thelma and Louise HAD done this before, Kristal said. They knew some boy who lived about a mile from us, and they wanted to visit him. I know this may sound like I think my child is perfect, but Kristal said they had talked her into it. She had gone along because Thelma and Louise were cool and she wanted to fit in. Classic story, right?

But Kristal had recognized Jerry's truck and knew he'd seen them on the road, knew she'd get in BIG trouble for being out alone.

"I kept telling them that we had to go," she said, "but they wouldn't leave, so I finally left by myself. They walked half a block behind me and laughed all the way home."

Kristal had been out there on the dark country road in the pouring Washington rain, on her own at 1 in the morning. A mother's worst nightmare. Well, at least it was the worst nightmare I'd had at the time.

In the end, what Kristal had endured that night taught her enough of a lesson so I didn't even punish her. She never spent much time with those girls after that.

9
IT'S BACK!

After about six months of being a normal kid, the world crashed down around our ankles.

"The leukemia is back," Dr. Dan said in the clinic one Friday, delivering the news that left our faith quivering. He ordered her back into the hospital and put together another protocol of chemotherapy.

"What???" Kristal and I said in unison.

We were shocked. Devastated. It was an enormous blow to our faith. Back in the hospital, we talked about it continually.

"If I was wrong about this…" Kristal began, sitting in the familiar white bed, "if God didn't really heal me, what else am I wrong about? This is so hard. It's just not fair!"

"No, it's not fair. But life isn't fair, honey, you know that," I said, twirling a strand of her three inches of hair. "Just look at my gorgeous daughter and all those lesser ones out there."

"I'm serious, Mom. What if God really doesn't exist? Doesn't care? What if this stuff kills me?"

"Honey, I don't believe He'd do that to either one of us. I'm absolutely convinced that He loves us. I've felt that too many times, too many ways to wonder about that. I don't get it either, don't know why this is back. It does seem like a dirty trick, but I'm going to give Him the benefit of the doubt. If He healed you once He can do it again."

"But why do I have to go through this again?"

"I don't know, but I choose to hang on. I'm sure God has a plan somewhere in this."

All I could do was hold her. I had no answers.

Friends tried to help. To explain it away. Some Christians didn't help at all. One told me that if I'd had enough faith, the leukemia wouldn't have come back. She marched us off to her church full of faith healers. But the leukemia didn't budge.

Another had the nerve to ask me where Kristal had sinned to have caused this.

"Give me a break!" I answered, incensed. "She's only 15! She hasn't had TIME for any major sin in her life."

Another said she'd had a vision of Kristal with demons crawling up and down her throat. I ask you, what was I supposed to DO with that? It was not at all helpful.

It was my friend and employee, Sharon, who sang to the Lord while she vacuumed, who gave me something to hang onto. She continually wrote out Scriptures to encourage us. She showed me a Scripture that said Satan was our enemy, that he used to be an angel who got greedy so God kicked him out of heaven. Sharon explained that his goal is to kill and destroy those who love God.

"Satan never wins but he is smart," she explained. "Smart enough to give you the same disease all over again. He wants to discourage you, to make you doubt. If he can pull you away from the Lord, he gets his way."

Some friends fell away—both Kristal's and mine. Her girlfriends had gotten out of the habit of stopping by. My friends still brought dinner by and I knew they were praying, but they had quit asking me to meet them for lunch or go to a movie. They'd all been very supportive when Kristal was first sick. They'd celebrated with us when the leukemia retreated. But people tend to look away from ugliness. As much as they rubberneck at accident scenes, very few people can look at burns or compound fractures or a child with cancer without wincing. And let's face it, facing the horrors of life gets old.

Makes people want to run in the other direction.

It's like people think that rottenness will rub off on them. Now that Kristal's leukemia was back, they might have to think of their own beliefs differently too. Maybe they just don't know what to say to someone in the center of a tragedy. For whatever reason, people sometimes went the other way when they saw us in the grocery store aisle. It's not that they didn't care. They just couldn't look.

Even though I tried to stay positive, my heart broke for Kristal. She had her head in the emesis basin again. She spent her days in that big white bed with the head and feet that went up and down. I spent a lot of midnight hours in the hospital chapel again. Talking to the Lord was the most peaceful part of my day, but I often just wanted to run and hide. To let the seat belt hold me until I calmed down.

As much as he hated hospitals, Gary once decided he'd relieve me and spend the night with her. Kristal was excited and sent Jeff and me home before her dad even arrived. Although I was dying to know how they were doing, I made myself leave them alone. She called about 10 P.M.

"Dad got here about seven," she said, her voice getting softer with each word. "Then he decided he'd go out for a few minutes. I thought we might talk, but he's still not back."

What could I say? How could I comfort her from so far away?

As much as I tried to think positively and believe despite the circumstances, my faith had been rocked too by the reappearance of this ugly disease. I'd heard that Christians were supposed to praise God in everything—whether good or bad. Tough assignment. How could I praise Him for bringing leukemia back? I didn't really believe He had caused it. Satan did that, but God allowed it. Allowed Satan to pull this dirty trick. That was the part that bugged me. If He was in control of the entire world and everything in it, then why would He allow this to happen to us?

I'd gotten into the habit of asking Him the tough questions at night, after the kids were tucked in for the night. When we were at the hospital, I went to the chapel, at home I went for a walk under the stars.

So far from the city, it was quiet, it was gorgeous. Looking up at a blanket of twinkling, bright stars, it was hard to feel like I was the center of the universe. As long as I kept looking up rather than at my circumstances, believing was a whole lot easier.

One night as I was talking—well, complaining might be a more appropriate word—to God about my list of issues and problems, I heard a soft prompt to look up. Above, the moon was a perfect semi-circle. It looked like some samurai warrior had used a big sword to lop it right in half.

"See that moon?" I heard God ask in the gentle way He always whispered to my spirit.

"Yes…"

"You believe that it's round, right? Even though you can't see the whole thing?"

"Of course I do," I thought, feeling silly.

"Trust me in this," He said, and I could almost feel His arm around my shoulders as He spoke. "Just the way you believe the other half of the moon is up there—even when you can't see it—I want you to believe, to know, that I'm working on your behalf."

I nodded and walked back in the house where I slept like a baby.

Perhaps that's why I liked to talk to God before I went to bed. It was like He slipped the backpack of worries from my shoulders and set it down at His feet. I tended to pick up the backpack again in the morning and fill it with rocks during the day, but at least it was empty for a while. Maybe that's why I need to pray every day, I thought.

It astounded me that God Himself is available to me 24

hours a day. Whenever I need to talk, He is there to listen until I'm finished. That had never happened with any mortal man.

SUMMER OF INFECTION

Kristal had made it through her sophomore year and another round of chemo when the summer of infection began. While her friends were out water skiing, learning to drive and talking about boyfriends, she was stuck in the hospital for another six weeks.

"I just want to be a normal kid again," she said again and again.

But in one department, she'd seemed pretty normal to me. Just like every other almost 16-year-old, Kristal wanted her driver's license. She had gotten her learner's permit and I'd begun teaching her to drive. My only car was my baby blue Ford Bubblegum van. It was big and boxy and when I wasn't hauling boxes or people, it echoed inside. It worked great for fashion shows because I'd had a clothing rod installed across the back so all the outfits arrived perfectly pressed.

I'd customized the outside too. When I'd ordered it, I'd had 16-inch round bubble windows installed on both sides. I found a sign company to paint the base of my bubblegum machine logo under the windows, so it looked like a real bubblegum machine. Then, in a stroke of genius that would have made Martha Stewart proud, I used chicken wire to trap about 200 colorful small plastic balls inside the bubble windows. The fact that the bubblegum balls slid around when I turned corners was a huge bonus. Kids loved that part.

It stuck out in a parking lot, to say the least. The van

was great advertising for the store, but on the down side, everyone in town knew where I was at all times. Good thing I never snuck around.

Kristal liked driving the van because it sat so high and she could see everything from the seat. We found empty parking lots and out of the way spots so she could practice driving. Then one day I let her drive home. She did great, even with other people on the road.

"Pull over and pick up the mail, will you?" I said as we were coming around the corner and down the hill toward the house. This feat required driving onto the left side of our country road, then making a 180-degree turn into our driveway. It also required slowing down, which I had evidently failed to mention.

She came in a little fast. Got a little close. Forgot about the big mirror that stuck out the side.

"Whoa!" Kristal yelled, ducking and stomping on the brakes at the same time. I'm sure I was yelling too as I covered my head.

Blue plastic newspaper holders (ours and the neighbor's) shattered as if she'd stuck a firecracker in them. Pieces flew in every direction. And the glossy black metal mailbox I had so carefully painted daisies on? It hung by two screws from the wooden stand. Even the neighbor's box was flattened.

"Cool!" Jeff yelled from the back seat.

Once the dust cleared, we all cracked up and sat there laughing like idiots.

"That's gotta be worth at least ten points!" I told her. We got out to assess the damage and found it was totally fixable, even with our limited skills. The wooden stand was a little wobbly but even my five-year-old car guy couldn't find any damage to the van. We climbed back in.

"Now, take a deep breath and s-l-o-w-l-y make the turn for the driveway. They call this an S-turn for a reason."

Obviously, it would take a few more lessons before she was ready to take her driving test. My kids were so used to cleaning up their own messes that I didn't have to tell her. As soon as she parked the van, she grabbed the hammer to go fix things as best she could. When Jeff took the hammer from her hand, I knew he'd do most of the straightening. Then I made her call the newspaper company to report the mishap. Luckily, they laughed too and said they'd replace the newspaper boxes.

She had to wait to get her driver's license, and finally took the test in a friend's car instead of my van. Soon afterward, her dad surprised her with a very used, rust-colored Chevy she named The Boat. My insurance man patted the five-foot-long hood and announced, "This is THE car every teenager should drive! There's so much metal around her that she'll never get hurt in an accident."

Meanwhile, Kristal had gone into remission a second time. Yes, we celebrated but not like the first time and not for long.

The other cancer hanging over my head was my divorce. I'd finally found a lawyer, filed papers and waited the required time. For the kids' sake, I tried to keep it to myself and not make a big deal of it. I didn't think Jeff would notice any change in his daily life. But when I put on a skirt and heels to go to court that morning, Kristal knew.

Jeff had been invited to the zoo with some friends from church and Joan said she'd check in on Kristal while I was gone. I think they both worried that I'd return in a white jacket with the sleeves tied in back. The preparation had taken a lot longer than the actual court date, but this whole thing was just a formality in my mind. Jerry and I had really been separate since the day he left the house more than a year earlier.

Still, Kristal and Joan spent the day making up songs to

cheer me up when I got back to the hospital. They managed to make this sad failure almost fun.

Shortly after Kristal's second remission, she began to run a fever. The dangers of a fever had been drilled into our heads. We knew that fevers usually mean infections and infections kill leukemia patients.

We'd been warned about fevers and been told to get our fannies to the hospital if her temperature ever hit 101. So when Kristal started to run a fever we went in. Again. This was about the 20th time she'd been admitted, so we knew the drill. But after a week, doctors still couldn't determine what was causing her high temps, which often soared to 104 degrees in the evenings.

My friend Judy put together a round-the-clock prayer chain. She called everyone at church to ask if they'd pray for Kristal for an hour. People signed up for times that would work for them, but then something strange happened.

"It was the funniest thing," she said. "Carolyn called me back. She said that 4-5 P.M. wasn't enough of a sacrifice. She and Don wanted to change their time. She asked if they could take 4-5 A.M. instead. Then someone else did the same thing. After that I had no trouble at all filling every single slot."

I had never really understood the term *church family* before that. These people, these wonderful, giving, praying, caring people of all ages and walks of life had become more like family to me than my biological family. I didn't hear from my own siblings for months at a time, yet DeeDee often stopped by with a big smile and the latest news. Helen brought dinner. Pastor Andy dropped by to pray for us. It seemed someone was always surprising me just because they cared.

Even with occasional help, Kristal's sickness was hard on all of us. Just like every other single mother out there, I was always overwhelmed with the number of responsibilities. Adding cancer to the list raised my stress level to about 112 on a scale of one to ten. I never finished everything on my list, never felt up to the task. The strain of running a business I couldn't spend much time on, trying to be there for Jeff, and protect my daughter while she rode a seesaw between life and death was not conducive to peace and tranquility.

Every other weekend, Jeff stayed with his dad. But most nights, he and I still slept on futons on the floor in Kristal's hospital room. During morning doctor's rounds, I'd sneak down the hall in my pajamas and into the parent's shower. Then I'd get Jeff ready for school, do my hair, kiss Kristal goodbye and drive the half hour to school, then head to the store.

After work, I dropped by the house to pick up clean clothes on the way back to the hospital. I could recite the hospital menu word for word. Sometimes we didn't spend more than a few hours at home all week.

My kitchen floor hadn't been scrubbed for months. I became increasingly glad I'd bought carpet to match the dirt in my back yard. Laundry accumulated until I couldn't justify grabbing the kids another new outfit from the store.

And my poor yard. My ex-husband is a Japanese gardener at heart and had spent every weekend humming along with lawnmowers and trimmers. What friends used to refer to as the "National Park" now looked more like a jungle. Since Jerry had been gone, the yard had frolicked back to its wild state. Roses grew leggy. Rhododendrons ran amuck. A layer of moss sprouted on the roof. Horsetails were as high as an elephant's eye. Boxes, bicycles and old hula hoops seemed to be multiplying out behind the garage.

One day at church, my friend Judy asked, "What can I do to help?"

She must've caught me at a weak moment. Before I even thought about it, I told her the truth. Normally, I'd flash a practiced faith-and-joy-in-all-circumstances smile and tell people I was okay. Friends regularly told me to call them if I needed anything, but who were they kidding? I was much too proud to actually call anyone to ask for help! No one had persisted enough to follow up.

But for some reason, this time I rattled off a long list of things to be done around the house and told her to take her pick. When she asked me to make her a list, I was surprised but not optimistic, thinking of her as another well-intentioned friend. After a few days, I had forgotten all about it.

About two weeks later as I drove down my steep, S-shaped driveway on a Saturday afternoon, my mouth flew open. Cars jammed my driveway. People swarmed everywhere. At least 25 people, some I had seen but never talked to at church, were busy doing all the things I never had time to do.

Staring in disbelief, I pulled the van into the only empty spot. There were men sweeping my roof, women shining windows, kids from the youth group carrying piles of brush to a burn pile. Chatter and laughter rang out from all corners of what was again looking like a National Park. When they saw my surprise and my tears, they all whooped and hollered like they were having a ball!

On the deck, the picnic table was filled with donuts and goodies. The smell of coffee wafted from a giant urn and mixed with the smell of freshly cut grass. Their camaraderie reminded me of the barn-raising parties I'd seen on *Little House on the Prairie*. They cleaned every walk and gutter, trimmed every bush, pulled every horsetail, hauled every piece of garbage to the dump. I got and gave 25 hugs that day but what was even more valuable was the lesson I learned.

The joy I saw on my friends' faces told me they were glad to have a practical way to help. I was so touched. So humbled. It still blesses me to think that the Lord had rearranged the lives of all these people just to bless me. I've never felt so special and spoiled.

What a revelation—they really did want to help! And all I had to do was admit I needed it. Lord knew I didn't have a gardener or the money to pay one. He could've sent one along any time, but He waited until I asked. My faith and trust grew 25-fold that day and maybe, just maybe, I could risk honesty and humility to ask the next time I had a crisis.

Just like the Lord, I thought. He is too kind to push anything on us, to force us to do anything. He waits patiently for us to ask.

Kristal was still in the hospital, still waiting for her fevers to let up. During the day, her temperature stayed in the 101-102 range, but evenings it spiked to 105-106 degrees. She slept much of the time and got weaker and weaker. I knew how draining it was to have a little temperature with a cold or the flu, so I couldn't imagine how she could survive weeks of this. But it went on and on and on—for nearly six weeks. Kristal got so weak I nearly had to carry her, IV cart and all, to the bathroom.

Doctors tested every little bit of her. She didn't have any open sores. Her lungs were fine. No sinus infection. They even checked her teeth to make sure she didn't have cavities. When they couldn't find the infection, they thought it must be hiding deep inside.

They finally decided that the infection might have something to do with her Hickman line. As a precaution, they planned to remove it. The day she was scheduled for surgery, I left my futon on the floor at 6 A.M. because of the complicated, tightly scheduled day ahead of me. I needed to drop Jeff off at a friend's and check in at the store before heading back to the hospital. And I was desperate for a hot shower and clean clothes.

Jeff and I raced home, thankfully headed in the

direction opposite most of the traffic. I threw a load of clothes in the washer, sent Jeff to the freezer for some hamburger to thaw for dinner and jumped into the shower. As I pulled on my blouse afterwards, he handed me the meat.

"I think there's something wrong with the freezer," he said, handing it to me. "This hamburger isn't hard."

This is all I need! I thought, counting the years since we had bought the noisy second-hand monster. And I had just filled it with meat! Muttering under my breath, I marched downstairs with water still dripping from my hair.

The smell of fish hit me as I flung open the freezer door. Gingerly I reached in and poked a salmon, which gave way under my fingers. Bread, turkey and beef—everything was soft; still cold, but definitely thawed. I slammed down the lid and pounded the top of it with clenched fists.

"Aaaaaagh!" I fumed. "How could this happen, today of all days? It isn't fair! I can't take any more!"

I stomped the floor with my bare feet. "Lord," I screamed up at the ceiling, "You promised not to give me any more than I could handle! You promised! Well, this is more than I can handle! You need to take something away!"

My mind and heart were filled to overflowing and, as usual, the excess spilled out of my mouth. I listed all of my problems out loud—and I mean really loud. There I was, jumping up and down and yelling, in a full-blown, toddler-worthy temper tantrum.

After several minutes, I fell to my knees, sobbing hysterically on the thinly carpeted cement floor, my tears pooling with the drips from my hair. I had taken as much as I could take.

Finally, though, I could scream no longer, and my fit subsided. I settled down in both body and spirit. Lying motionless, exhausted, crumpled on the floor, I tried to regroup.

Then, as if it had gotten to the end of a long-held

breath, there came the sound of an unmistakable clunk, followed by a familiar hummmm. I looked up. I got back up on my knees. I could hardly believe my ears. That old freezer's motor had restarted!!

I had hated that sound for years. It was audible from upstairs every time it kicked in, a noisy reminder of the lousy $25 we spent on it. This time, though, it sounded like the voices of angels.

I stared in disbelief. It continued to hum along as if it didn't have a problem in the world. Still on my knees, I began to cry again. This time, though, my tears were for the love and faithfulness of the Lord. Gratefulness filled my soul. I had demanded that God do something (I couldn't exactly call it a prayer now could I?) yet He responded anyway. I was a brat, not at all worthy of His attention. Yet He answered. He saved the day. One more time, He saved the day.

With my heart overflowing, I got up, went back upstairs, and stumbled on with my day. And the old freezer? It eventually died for good. About a year later, as I recall. On a much less complicated day.

Even after the surgery to remove Kristal's central line, her fevers didn't subside. Something else freaked us out too. It looked like Kristal was developing holes in the skin of the palms of her hands and the soles of her feet.

As she ate a little packet of chocolate pudding one day, the handle of her spoon kept getting stuck in the loose skin of her palm. A few days later, thick pieces of skin started peeling away from her palms and her feet. She'd peel it back and we'd cut it off to get it out of the way. She said it felt like a peeling sunburn so it didn't hurt, but it sure looked weird.

"Maybe I could be a hand model," she said, waving her hands through the air with skin dangling from them. "You know, in one of those horror movies! Wooo-ooo. I could make a fortune!"

We laughed at the absurdity of it all, although this palms and soles peeling is apparently normal for people who have sustained high fevers. I know it's a little gross, but I still have a solid two-inch square chunk of skin from her heel.

II
SWEET 16

As the fevers continued, so did the calendar. It kept creeping toward August 14, Kristal's birthday. She would be 16 years old.

"How would you like to celebrate? This is a big deal, you know!"

"I think I'll skip this one if you don't mind."

"That's what old women always say. You're only 16! We have to have a party—how about a Sweet 16 party?"

"I'm not feeling very sweet right now," she said, rolling over and closing her eyes.

"So, what kind of cake should I bake? Want the usual chocolate with peanut butter frosting?"

But Kristal refused to get into it. I kept thinking that she'd pull out of this funk if her friends all showed up to celebrate with her. So, I planned a party anyway. Neen, Shirley and Caroline, who all worked at the Bubblegum Closet, created an incredible car out of cardboard. Using a kind of paper mache, Caroline created a 36-inch tall, baby blue vehicle complete with headlights and on and off switches on the dashboard. They even made aluminum foil keys for the ignition! I wish I could say that Kristal loved it. She looked at it briefly, said it was cute, then rolled over and went back to sleep. Even at her own party, she couldn't stay awake.

All of the 60 people who showed up got the same

treatment. They probably thought she was rude or ungrateful, but since most of them hadn't seen her in quite a while, they had no idea how sick she really was. My mom and dad called to wish her a happy birthday too, but she fell asleep two sentences into the conversation. I think that scared them.

While we had been facing this swirl of madness, my parents had been traveling, visiting family in South Dakota. In the winter, their motor home stayed parked at their retirement home in Arizona; in the summer they used it to see the country and visit friends. But after the birthday incident, they decided to turn the motor home around and come to help me. This decision nearly caused my head to whip around and fall from my neck.

I had not asked. I never asked them for help. Hadn't since I started working at 15. My mother had taught me that there was something seriously wrong with anyone who couldn't handle things on her own. In my family, you didn't flinch—even if a big missile like leukemia hit you right between the eyes.

But let's face it—it was hard, killer hard, to keep up these days. Hard to be there for everyone. Hard to decide who would need me more each day. If there had been time to be honest with myself, I would have realized that Kristal's fever was draining me nearly as much as it was her.

Kristal hadn't eaten solid food for weeks and was down to under 100 pounds. All that time spent lying in bed had caused her muscles to atrophy and she was so weak. Her skin was nearly transparent and stretched tightly over her 5'6" skeleton. Those great cheekbones were back but it nearly broke my heart to be able to clearly see and feel every rib and backbone. She was so weak that she stumbled and swayed like an old, old woman.

Four days after my parents' phone call, Dad swung the motor home into the hospital parking lot. In his congenial way, he tracked down the security department and arranged to park there and even plug in to their electricity. Mom offered to take over the night shift so I could sleep in my own bed for a while. Poor woman hadn't yet met the two-inch foam mattress on the hospital floor.

Shortly after they arrived, doctors finally found a bacterial infection in Kristal's blood. They put her on a different antibiotic and she soon began to raise her head from the pillow once in a while. She was clearly feeling better.

One day Mom asked me to go to the coffee shop with her. Weird, since neither of us drank coffee. We slid into the booth and made small talk for a few minutes before she got to what she wanted to tell me.

"God spoke to me last night," she said in a whisper.

"No kidding?" I responded, thinking she might really be kidding. "What did He say?"

"Well, I was just laying there praying for Kristal when He said He wanted my heart."

"Cool! What'd you tell Him?"

"Well, what'd'ya think? I told Him, 'Okay.'"

It was so simple! I had prayed for my mom since I learned to pray. She had grown up in the Lutheran Church, went to church for all of her 58 years, yet she'd never heard the part about having a relationship with Jesus. Now, just like that, my mom had given her heart to Him. I was ecstatic, but since jumping and down excitement wasn't permitted in my family, I couldn't show my enthusiasm. Even after many years, I still love twirling the thought in my mind, saying it out loud—"My mother met the Lord in Kristal's hospital room." It seemed pretty close to a miracle to me.

After Kristal's bacterial infection cleared up, they reinserted her Hickman central line so nurses could hook her IV line up to liquid nutrition every night. Mom was still spending nights at the hospital, and I was surprised to watch my daughter and my mother become good friends. They'd been close when she was little, but it had been some time since I had arrived in a room to find them laughing. That was something that rarely happened between my mother and me. Kristal became kind of a buffer between us.

When Kristal was finally released from the hospital, the summer was nearly over. Mom and Dad waved goodbye and headed for Arizona.

One day during a checkup, Joan told us that our friend Clayton, who had a little crush on Kristal, had been in the ICU for several days. They wouldn't let Kristal in ICU, but I went down to see him. He was asleep and all alone in a 10x10 room stuffed full of beeping and whirring machines—all hooked up to him. His kidneys were shutting down again and couldn't handle the fluid in his body. He looked more like a Sumo wrestler than the sweet and charming 12-year-old he was.

I once told Clayton that he made me wonder more about God than anyone I'd ever met. I knew God was capable of snapping His mighty fingers and totally healing any old liver. So why didn't He do that? Why do innocents all over the world get sick? I'd heard that disease came into the world when Satan was kicked out of heaven and put in charge of this earth, but still. Why was it necessary for Clayton to live the way he did, to suffer the way he did? It's one of the questions I'd like to ask Jesus when I get to Heaven myself.

While I was looking around the ICU for Clayton's mom, the hospital Chaplain appeared around a corner, so we went to the end of the hall to talk. He and I spoke often, and he was very close to Clayton as well.

"Clayton told me he had a dream last night," he said. "He said he was tired from walking when he came to a big gate. He didn't know where it led, but knew he needed to get inside. But the doors were too heavy to open. The gate was too tall, and he couldn't find anything to climb on.

He jumped and jumped but couldn't reach the big, heavy handle. He remembers falling, exhausted and sweating, in front of the gate.

"He wanted to know what I thought it meant. I told him I thought that his gate was the gate to Heaven."

"Really?" I said, on the edge of my seat. "What'd he say?"

"He nodded for a few seconds, then said that made sense. So, I told him just how to get in that door."

"No kidding! I've been trying to talk to him about this for so long! What did you say?"

"I told him he just had to believe in Jesus with all his heart and ask His forgiveness. 'Na, it can't be that easy,' Clayton said. I told him I knew it was hard to believe, but that it really WAS that easy.

"'Do you really want to live forever in that beautiful place you saw?' I asked him. He said he did, then he prayed with me. I gave him a few simple instructions—to tell God that he was sorry for his sins, that he believed Jesus was God's son and died for those sins, and that he wanted to live with Him in heaven.

"Clayton opened his eyes, looked around the room and said, 'That was simple. Think it worked?' That kid cracks me up! I just nodded and told him I knew it did. You know—when he was done, his sallow skin seemed a little bit brighter. And you know Clayton—that smile just got broader and broader."

I was so excited for him! Clayton's name was now written in that big book of God's. This kid had been in and out of the hospital for years. He'd had several kidney transplants. His kidneys would work for a while, but within a year or two he'd be on dialysis again. He had never been able to run and play with the kids in his classes. He'd never known the joy of the wind in his hair while he whizzed along on a bike. I had wondered how Clayton's mother had walked through all of this by herself for the last decade. I'd tried to tell her, but she had no idea she could lean on the Lord.

A few times over the years she'd tried to get a job but the state said they'd take her boys away if she wasn't there to care for them. Twice she'd broken engagements with decent, honorable men because the state threatened to cancel their health insurance. Donald Trump would have complained about having to pay Clayton's medical bills. His health issues had ruled Cindy's life.

"Does Cindy know about Clayton's new faith?" I asked.

"He told her about the dream, but I don't know about anything else."

I found out that Clayton had had another dream the next night. This time he approached the same imposing gate, but he now knew how to open it. He just called the name of Jesus and the gate swung open. He was in Heaven!

"It was a big, big field, Mom, with beautiful green grass and flowers," he excitedly told his mom the next morning. "I could run, Mom! I ran down the hill so fast. And I could ride my bike! It was so great!"

Clayton died that day. He didn't hurt any more. His kidneys worked just fine. For the first time in his life, he could keep up with all the other kids. I think he lived just long enough to let his mother know about Heaven, to let her know he'd be okay.

And the day after that, Cindy called me with a request.

"Nothing fits Clayton," she said, "and I don't have anything to bury him in. He was so bloated. Do you have anything that would work? I have no idea what size he is."

I thought Clayton might need something from the men's department rather than anything I carried, but I drove to the store to scour the racks. I'd dressed all kinds of children for all kinds of weddings, birthdays and big, fancy parties. But as I pulled out a size 18-20 blue sweat suit with a wide stripe and a loose, stretchy waistband, I knew I'd just chosen the most important outfit of my career.

All those perfect little dresses and suits I'd sold over the years melted into one big who-cares-sort-of-pile. It was a much bigger honor to choose the outfit that Clayton wore when he walked through that big golden gate to meet his King.

12
MIRACLE
AFTER MIRACLE

Even though we were in the middle of another busy back-to-school season at the store, the more time Kristal spent in the hospital, the more broke I got. For over a year now, I'd been paying people to take my place at the store. Neen carried the bulk of the responsibility and managed the part-time employees but, perhaps because Gig Harbor is a small town, customers expected me to be there whenever the neon bubblegum machine glowed in the window. For whatever reason, when I wasn't there, business suffered.

The store did its best to support us but by fall, money kept getting tighter. I was paying our bills out of the business, still trying to support my family on the proceeds. And as usual, between "back to school" and Christmas seasons, I needed more inventory than I carried the rest of the year— about $40,000 more.

Because retail stores have to pay for merchandise 30 days after it arrives, I was in the habit of borrowing $40,000 to purchase it, then paying back the bank on January 1. It was neat. Clean. And it had worked that way with the same just-across-the-parking-lot bank for a few years.

But this year my banker, Chuck, looked at my books, noticed my shrinking revenues and got nervous. Then I found out that he had invited Jerry to lunch to ask what he thought of my ability to repay this loan! I was livid!!

If Chuck had been as intuitive as a gray weasel, he

would have smelled his own tail burning when I got him on the phone. He reminded me that he and Jerry knew each other from the Kiwanis Club, then contritely admitted he'd consulted with him. Consorted with Jerry. Decided against the loan with Jerry! He excused the action of course, saying he had no idea that we were no longer together. He said he had simply thought that Jerry would know all about my business.

"Well, that's strange, Chuck," I told him, "because never once in all the years we've worked together have you called me to discuss HIS business." Then I hung up on the little creep.

So I had no loan, no money. And UPS was delivering huge stacks of boxes of new merchandise every day. I applied for a loan at a couple of other banks, but my only financial relationship had been with the up-to-that-point faithful Chuck. They all said no. So I had $40,000 worth of merchandise I wouldn't be able to pay for until people finished their Christmas shopping—long after the bills came due.

At least Kristal was home from the hospital after her horrible summer. She had trouble keeping her eyes open so obviously we were back to the tutors because she was nowhere near well enough to attend school.

She did, in her infirmity, have the greatest cheekbones I've ever seen. With her skin as pale and fine as porcelain, she looked stunningly beautiful. Her long ordeal with chemotherapy, surgery and a blood infection left her with the energy of a rag doll. She was down to a skeletal 84 pounds. She couldn't eat anything. No favorite dinners, no pizza, no pickles, not even gum. She couldn't keep a single thing down.

Out of necessity, I became her home health care nurse. Every night I hooked her up to an IV and fed her lipids (fats, which look like heavy cream) and Total Parenteral Nutrition, or TPN, (which is a mixture of vitamins and nutrients but looks like pee.) Not an appetizing brew, but it kept her alive. Literally. I would gladly have paid more than the hundreds of dollars a day I knew the stuff cost.

Anyway, the debts mounted as the days wore on, and I continued to pray for wisdom. I began to consider closing the store. Even though health insurance was miraculously paying 90% of the hospital bills, my 10% was coming close to bankrupting me. I was more fortunate than many single moms—both Jerry and Gary had always been faithful at paying their child support. But even added together, that only covered a portion of the mortgage. I didn't see any way to pay the utilities, phone and food, which all seemed pretty necessary, but I also hated the very idea of bankruptcy. Walking away and letting someone else pay off my bills was against everything I'd ever been taught. This huge dilemma weighed on me almost as heavily as Kristal's health, well, lack of health. Some days I felt like I was drowning under enormous waves that refused to let up.

I finally asked my brother-in-law, who was vice-president of a large corporation, for advice. Jon offered to help me put together a financial plan so I could apply for another loan. He poured over my books, which were looking worse by the day. Then I didn't hear from him for two weeks.

I knew if I didn't close store soon, someone else would close it for me. I prayed, as I always did these days, and God gave me a final date. I was so sad about the thought, but I didn't tell a soul. It was between me and Him.

About 8 o'clock on the night before I was planning to make "going out of business" signs, Jon called. He told me casually that he had just put a $40,000 check in the mail to me. For a second, I couldn't speak, couldn't move.

"But I didn't ask for a loan," I stammered.

I felt a gigantic bubble of relief and gratitude burst inside of me and come pouring out in a stream of gratitude. But Jon didn't seem to expect or want any of that. He simply said he thought it was a good investment.

I was stunned. Oh, so grateful that someone would believe in me, come alongside me and help. I cried for more than an hour. I hadn't asked Jon to loan me the money. But I guess God had decided it was not time to close the Bubblegum Closet, so He provided a way to keep it open.

Although Jon didn't believe in God, I knew God believed in Jon—enough to ask him to help. It took hours to write out $40,000 worth of checks, but it felt soooo good to pay off my debts. To this day, I still pray blessings on Jon for his generosity. And I pray that Jon recognizes that his good fortune comes from God.

So, the financial pressure was relieved that fall, but Kristal was not getting better. She was still weak as a kitten, and looked as starved as one too but she still wouldn't eat. Couldn't eat. I didn't understand which it was, but the result was the same. Kerry or Deanna or Kim sometimes stopped to visit after school, but it would be a long time before Kristal could join them there. Every night, I used my osmosis nursing degree and hooked up her to the cream and pee cocktail that somehow made its way from her bloodstream to her stomach to keep her alive.

My good friends Bob and Jeani, who had helped introduce me to the Lord were teachers. They teamed up with Madge, who had once co-coached the third and fourth grade softball team with me, and asked the community to help. In secret, they came up with a multi-faceted plan.

First, they created Kristal tickets. I don't remember exactly what they bought or how they worked, but I was at work when I heard about it.

"Have you been across the street?" a good customer

asked when she came into the store one day.

"No, should I? What's going on?" I asked.

"There's a bunch of high school kids selling Kristal tickets in front of the grocery store. I hear they're selling them in the school lunchroom too."

"What? What do you mean?"

"They're raising money to help with Kristal's medical bills."

I was stunned. Stunned. Just imagine this—kids standing in front of grocery stores asking people to buy tickets to help raise money for your child! Emotions slithered through me. I was honored, embarrassed, and humbled all at the same time. Honored to be the mother of someone who people cared about enough to help. Embarrassed because my upbringing forbid asking for help. And humbled because everyone knew I was the one who needed help.

In previous years, I'd been the giver. The one people came to for help. The Bubblegum Closet had supported Little League and bowling teams, given outfits to kids who needed them, helped send kids to Washington DC and beauty pageants and bought Christmas wreaths from the Boy Scouts and cookies from the Girl Scouts. I loved giving. It felt good to be able to help—like I was a hero or something. It feels great to offer someone something they don't have.

But being on the receiving end was new for me. Made me squirm like my pants were full of spiders.

Turns out that Bob and Jeani had sent out a letter to all the other teachers in the school district, telling them about Kristal and what she was going through. We found out about it when they showed up with an enormous basket full of handmade cards and tear-tugging letters, all in varying degrees of childhood penmanship. Some were decorated in hearts and lace, some had been lettered in Magic Marker because their fingers were too small to hold a pen.

"Get well," was a common theme.

"Eat your Wheaties," one suggested.

"I love you."

"Come back to school."

Kristal spent days reading and rereading each and every one.

"These letters are so sweet!" Kristal said, her lap full of cards. "I can't believe this many kids took time to write to me."

She loved them and really appreciated that everyone cared. On the other hand, she had trouble with everyone knowing she was sick.

"It's embarrassing! I hate to be the center of attention, hate to have everyone thinking of me as 'that poor, sick girl!'" she complained.

Poor kid. I hadn't even realized that I'd passed along my boatload of pride.

They'd also scheduled a blood drive, so the local newspaper called to see if they could do a story. I knew these people, spent hundreds of dollars each month advertising in their paper. Because of the businesses, people knew Jerry and me in Gig Harbor. For years now, we'd both worked with the local business association and the Chamber of Commerce. Even though Kristal was uncomfortable with this attention, I couldn't say no. They interviewed me, but Kristal refused to pose for photos.

"Tell them I'm too sick," she said, pulling the covers over her bratty face.

She said the same thing when Gig Harbor's Mayor declared a Kristal Day. A day in her honor for heaven's sake! The fundraising committee had been busy there too. They'd gone to every business in town to collect merchandise for an auction to be held at the nicest restaurant in town on—what else? Kristal Day, November 11, 1986. She wouldn't go.

"You go," she said, sending me to pick up the key to the city that the Mayor had engraved for her. "Tell them I'm not strong enough to be there. That I can't stay awake that late." That part was true.

So, I went to the auction alone. Car places offered free oil changes and lube jobs, restaurants and stores gave gift certificates, florists sent bouquets of flowers. Table after classy table was filled with donations. At least a hundred people were bidding and the auction went on and on and on. Everyone was so sweet and kind that I was in tears most of the night. Even Dixie Lee Ray, Washington State's governor, who happened to live on Fox Island, had sent a piece of her handmade jewelry. I couldn't believe that so many of my friends and colleagues—and many people I'd never heard of (who are the Bells?)—had gone to all this trouble to help us. It was so humbling, so touching, that it still brings me to tears to talk about it.

And by the end of the night, this dynamic team of friends had raised more than $8,000 to help with medical bills. $8,000! Their care was overwhelming. Absolutely overwhelming.

"Why did they DO all of this?" Kristal asked.

"Because they care," I told her. "Because people are good and they want to help. Because their children are not sick, and they're grateful for that. Because that's how the world works. They can't be here to help every day, but they can offer… "

"What do you mean?" she spat. "I hate needing to be taken care of."

"That's called pride, my dear. I hate it too, but I've learned that God hates pride so I'm trying to get over it. This is the way He'd like it to work—we give whenever we can, whenever people ask. And when we need it, we gracefully accept help. We humble ourselves. You know how great it feels to be able to help people? Just think about it this way— if you accept help, you're letting them feel that good."

"Yeah, okay. But I'd rather be on the other side. It's fun

to give someone a great new outfit or whatever, but it's awful to be the one in need. Embarrassing."

"Yeah, but right now we're in that spot. And aren't you glad we've given to others over the years? My mother used to say, 'What goes 'round comes 'round.' We get what we give in this life, you know?"

13
WINTER WOES

As the weather got colder, it was about to give us something we didn't generally see. The Seattle area has a moderate climate and lots of hills. One or two snows a year are normal, and they usually fall and melt within 24 hours. But if the cold sticks around, as it did in 1986, even an inch or two of snow can freeze at night, turning hills and bridges into giant skating rinks. It's fun to sled, but treacherous to drive. This year, it snowed and it snowed and it snowed again.

That presented us with two problems. First, we knew that if Kristal's temperature ever got as high as 101, we had to get her to the hospital, pronto. Infections of any kind, even from a simple cold, kill leukemia patients. Second, my darling Bubblegum van absolutely hated snow. Even with snow tires and the back end filled with firewood, she fishtailed and scooted and slid, but stubbornly refused to climb the numerous hills between our house and where I wanted to go. Needed to go—like to the hospital.

After dinner one night, we turned on the outdoor lights so Kristal and Jeff could watch snow pile up on the life-size cement seagull who sat, wings spread and ready to rise, on our deck. I was concerned because Kristal had been sneezing, and I'd heard her cough a couple of times. Her face was flushed, and I suspected that her temperature was rising. I'd been touching her face and forehead all day—sneakily of course, so she had no idea I was worried. At least that's what I told myself. As the hands of the clock crept toward 10 o'clock, I took her temperature. It was 100.5.

"We'll just watch it," I said, knowing that she understood the risks as well as I did. "I'm sure you'll be fine."

As children's temperatures seem to do, Kristal's kept climbing throughout the evening. By 11 o'clock, the little mercury deal was on the wrong side of 101. I knew I had to find someone to take us to the hospital but didn't know who to call. Perhaps my attitude harkened back to the *children are to be seen and not heard* from my childhood, but I couldn't make myself bother anyone. Kristal and I talked about it. And who did we know who had a four-wheel drive anyhow? I couldn't think of a soul.

Well, there was Steve, my friend's husband. If I called her, I knew she'd make him drive me. After all, who would refuse a leukemia patient? But I sometimes had a hard time with this guy who knew everything and sometimes went on and on about it. But at this hour, Kristal reminded me, as if I hadn't thought of it, he was probably sleeping. I couldn't call him now. Instead, we prayed and I changed cold cloths on Kristal's forehead.

The next time I checked it was 102. But if I hadn't had the guts to bother someone at 10 or 11, I certainly couldn't call at midnight. I felt terrible. I'd obviously found another pocketful of pride in my heart. Would I risk my child's health because I was unwilling to spend 32 minutes listening to unwelcome advice? Apparently so. We prayed again.

"God, I'm so weak," I said. "Please help us. Your Word says that You are the Great Physician. You know every cell of her body. We can't get to the doctor tonight, so will You please be Kristal's doctor? Will you bring down her temperature? Take away any infection. Keep her safe. I trust You, Lord."

Kristal had a lukewarm bath and we went to bed. But

I didn't sleep. I kept worrying, feeling like an idiot. Beating myself up. Idiot. Idiot! Praying.

"Get up and check her temperature," God whispered. Each time I listened these days, I recognized His voice a little easier. But I couldn't get up. I was afraid of what I'd find. He nudged me again. For over an hour I tossed and turned and argued the point. I think it was 2 A.M. before I obeyed.

Kristal's forehead was cool to my touch. I cried like a baby. I repented of my pride and unbelief. God, in His mercy, had not only brought down Kristal's temperature, but He wanted to protect me too. He had kept nudging me to get up. He wanted to reassure me, to let me get some sleep, yet it had taken me an hour to do what He asked. Would I ever get it right? I didn't deserve any kindness at all, but He gave it to me anyway. I smiled all the way back to bed.

That night, I swore that we would never again be at someone else's mercy. We needed a new car that could make it through the snow. But because of our tight budget, we'd have to wait a little longer.

Our driveway was steep, and so was the narrow road that approached it. The road ran right along the water and just before it got to our house, it rose sharply, then dipped enough to put butterflies in your stomach if you were in a hurry. Just before the dip, there was a 25-foot cliff on the water side with no guardrail.

Although I loved my Bubblegum van, this was not her year. Every time it was icy, she just spun and spun on the pavement until we eventually spun to the side of the road. More than once I had to abandon her there. People got used to seeing her there and no one ever hit her. One advantage was that another islander sometimes happened along, recognized us trudging through the drifts, and drove us home. The van just sat there until the snow melted. My van got lots of points for being cute, but her wimpiness made her a local joke.

One night when Kristal was safely ensconced in the

hospital, it started snowing. Since I knew it might last for days, Jeff and I decided to make a run for home. We stopped for groceries so we'd have something to eat if we were snowbound.

It was well after dark and we were getting so close that I kept patting the dashboard and telling my little van how proud I was of her. Then we got to the notorious hill just before the house. Even with six bags of groceries added to the firewood in the back, we couldn't get up that dratted little hill. We kept sliding to the right, dangerously close to the drop off at the side of the road. I had to leave her in that precarious position.

And the groceries would freeze if I left them in the car. I was exhausted and didn't want to go back after them either. So I loaded up Kristal's laundry, my purse and the grocery bags and locked it up. I handed Jeff a gallon of milk and a gallon of apple juice—the kind with the handles built into the plastic containers. He complained about their weight. Since I could already feel the plastic grocery store bags cutting into my hands, I needed him to help get the stuff up the hill, then down the other side. I probably yelled at him in the silent white night. Then, in the moonlight, I noticed tracks in the snow where someone in a decent snow vehicle had made it over the hill.

"Hey," I said when we reached the top, "I have an idea! Let's have a race! See these tracks? Put the milk in one and the apple juice in the other. When I yell Go! give them a shove. We'll see which is the fastest!"

Jeff jumped up and down, immediately revitalized. *Give the boy a game and he's happy*, I thought. We cheered when the milk won the race. When we got to our steep driveway though, there were no more tracks. Jeff kept trying to shove them down but they didn't want to slide on the powdery snow. Durable packaging, I marveled, as we finally made it home.

Anyway, after multiple fiascos involving my Bubblegum

van and snow banks, I decided we needed a new car. One incident helped me decide which kind.

One morning when my van was in one of those snow banks, I swallowed my pride and called Steve, who dutifully drove me to the hospital. All around us, other cars were slipping and spinning on the icy pavement, but Steve either bossed them out of his way or zipped around them. I held on to the door handle for dear life.

But the cool thing was that his Subaru never once slipped or slid on the ice. While we were whipping around the tight corner pulling onto the Narrows Bridge, I decided my next car would be a Subaru. I would never again be at the mercy of the weather. Or Steve.

14
BREAKING
HER FAST

Back at home, Kristal still wasn't eating. My eyes turned to her hopefully every time we sat down for dinner. I desperately wanted her to join us, to eat just a few tiny bites. But even when I served her favorites like pizza or spaghetti, I couldn't coax her into coming to the table. She was 5'6", yet her weight still hovered around 90 pounds. My once vibrant, bouncy teenager had shrunk to a weak and anemic willow stick with great cheekbones.

In response to my anxious looks, she'd say, "I think I'll be able to eat something tomorrow."

But I'd seen no signs to bolster such hope. Sure, the chemotherapy had killed the leukemia cells, but after a year of intermittent chemo, just thinking of food made her sick. I couldn't get her to try even a morsel. No meat, no fish, no vegetables, no fruit, no candy, no bread, no ice cream. Nothing.

That fall, I never gave up trying to get Kristal to eat meals with us. But how could she not pop a bite-sized Milky Way in her mouth at Halloween or try a bite of pumpkin pie at Thanksgiving?

The only thing sustaining Kristal was the very expensive bottles of liquid nutrients I hooked her up to every night. As I watched the life-giving fluid dripped into her veins, I wondered how long she could survive without eating. Sometimes I wondered how long I'd survive. How long could

I watch my daughter get weaker and weaker every day? Life sometimes seemed too difficult to bear. More times than I can count, I sat weeping and praying at my sleeping daughter's bedside.

"Help us, Lord," I would whisper into the darkness. "I feel like I'm sinking."

Christmas was racing toward us. Kristal was still not back in school, still not eating. The store was busy, but I was still broke from all of the hospital bills and I didn't know what I'd be able to buy the kids for Christmas. I kept thinking I'd bake the expected assortment of Christmas cookies, but hadn't even made sugar cookies with no decorations.

"When are we going to get our tree?" Jeff asked again and again.

Every Christmas of his life we had gone to Ketchum's Tree Farm and tromped through acres of property, usually in a drizzling rain, to cut down our own tree. Part of the experience was the haggling—not with Mr. Ketchum—with each other. We each chose a different tree and had great debates there among the pines to sell each other on the one we'd chosen. So, with Mt. Rainier as a backdrop, we spent a rare sunny Sunday afternoon finding our $10 tree.

"See that skinny little tree over there?" Kristal asked, leaning against the car while Jeff and I were deciding. "The one that looks like a Charlie Brown tree? That 's the one I want for my bedroom."

"Are you nuts? What is this with this tree in the bedroom again?"

"I love Christmas trees! They're so pretty. And we never use all the lights and stuff. I'll use whatever's left over."

"But I don't want you in your room all by yourself," I argued. "Christmas is a time to be together, with one tree. In the living room. You know…together. Besides, what if you forgot to turn it off at night or water it and it caught fire?"

And I didn't want to spend the money on another tree. She didn't push the point. But as soon as we got home Kristal and Jeff headed outside.

"What???" I said when they returned ten minutes later dragging a couple of five-foot branches. "Where did you get those?"

"In the yard," Jeff said, throwing his head in the air as if it was his idea. Kristal had done this before and now she had him convinced he needed one too.

"Okay, I give," I said, throwing up my hands. "Decorate them if you want, but no lights. They'll look good with some paper chains and stuff."

Moving slowly after an hour that exhausted her, Kristal helped Jeff find some paper and scissors while I went to the garage to find the rusty, awful Christmas tree stand. I had always hated this red and green contraption that could have been mistaken for a three-pronged bear trap.

Trying to get the tree into the stand while you hold it at the bottom and try to keep it upright while you turn those long screws into the trunk and get that sticky sap all over your hands sort of got to me. I could feel my blood pressure and my hackles rising.

"Hey, you guys. Get in here and help! I can't get this thing…"

Kristal held it upright while Jeff kept trying to give me advice. If I hadn't been right there in the room when he was born, I'd argue that he was at least 35. He had an uncanny way of seeing the logic of any situation. More than once while his dad was pulling our boat out of the water, I'd cringed when he walked over to a couple of grown men to tell them what they were doing wrong. And the weird part was that he was right.

But I was already in a tizzy and the screws had bitten two inches into the wood so I didn't want to listen to him any more than those guys who had a new $40,000 boat they couldn't get onto their trailer. I had to back the screws out and start over. We finally got the thing to stand up moderately straight, so we put water in the stand, then got some lights on it just as dusk hit. It did look pretty, twinkling there in the living room.

As soon as Jeff and I sat down to dinner though, Kristal yelled from her spot on the couch, "Hey, the treeeee..."

I got there just in time to pick it up and mop up the water on the carpet. Dinner got cold as we struggled to put the stupid thing back in the stand. It didn't fall again until we were sitting down to watch a movie.

The fourth time it happened, I grabbed the tree—lights and all—like a hand-held missile. The stand clung to the bottom like a scared little girl. I yanked open the sliding glass door and tossed it onto the deck, screaming all the while. Of course it caught before it got all the way out the door, because I hadn't pulled out the electrical cord, but you can still picture this, right? It was not pretty. My face was red, my eyes were beady and my poor kids had backed into the corner. I ran to my bedroom in tears.

I was sooo angry! This was too much! Where was my husband and why wasn't he putting up this stupid tree? Who was helping me pay the bills and mind the kids and carry this enormous load?

I threw myself onto the bed, ranting to God about being a single parent. I hated it! The load never lessened. It was Christmas for heaven's sake, and there was no one to help. I had twice as much responsibility as I wanted and half of the help, half of the money. The bills were still a mile high and I had no idea how I'd pay them.

God just listened patiently. It was like He was sitting there right beside me. My heartbeat returned to normal, and I calmed down. I don't know if it was His idea or not, but I began to ask myself some questions.

What am I doing wrong? Will I ever get it right?

I got into this mess, I decided, because of my own decisions. Not Kristal's leukemia, of course, but much of this mess was a consequence of my own stupidity. I hadn't listened when that voice in my heart warned me about marrying a man who dated two other women while we were engaged. That voice had been God's. And if I wasn't so proud, I could have invited someone to come help put up the tree. These things were my fault, not God's.

When I emerged from my room Jeff had the tree back up in the living room. He had found a five-gallon bucket, put the tree in it, and filled it with rocks and sand from the beach. I was so ashamed that all I could do was apologize for my insanity and cuddle my kids. We started the movie over and watched the entire thing without incident. That tree didn't move until we tossed it out in January.

This could have been the day I first said, "I don't need a husband, but I could sure use a handyman." From that day on, Jeff became my handyman.

But there was still the issue of Kristal not eating. It had been three full months since she'd put one single thing in her mouth. No wonder she was often weak and shaky.

I could not think of a single thing that would make her want to take a bite. Candy canes? Nope. Christmas cookies? Nope. Fudge? Nothing even tempted her. I was still feeding her the cream and pee cocktail every night.

The Bubblegum Closet's Christmas party tradition was a night out for the girls to thank them for their hard work. One evening between Christmas and New Year's Eve, we dressed up in our sequins and heels and went to the best restaurant in town. On the day of this year's reservation, Kristal and I were headed home from her checkup when I reminded her of the event.

"I wish I could go," she said, laying her head back on the headrest.

"What?" I said, incredulous. "Why? You don't eat. Why would you want to go out to dinner?"

"Well, I might eat," she said.

I'd heard this before. She often said she felt like eating something—usually something as specific as an Orange Crush in a glass bottle—only to let it sit there and go flat after I had searched all over town to find it.

I'm onto you, Missy, I thought, laughing. But she persisted.

"Maybe I'd eat a shrimp cocktail," she said dreamily.

"Okay. Fine," I said. "Come with us. You know Neen and Carolyn, and Shirley and Debbie... They'd love to see you. Even if you didn't eat, you'd have fun. Come along if you want."

So I found someone to watch Jeff and she did. She put on her best dress, spiked her two inches of blonde hair, and away we went to the Shorline (I'm not the only one in Gig Harbor who ever ignored a dictionary) Restaurant, an elegant place with a terrific view of the lighted boats in Gig Harbor Bay's marinas.

The table of eight yacky women went silent when Kristal ordered that shrimp cocktail. But when she used her long, perfect fingernails to raise a colossal shrimp from its precarious perch on the edge of a crystal compote, dunk it deep into the cocktail sauce, and take a bite, we all burst into tears. These women, who had daily stood beside me, daily heard about my struggles, daily cared about us as much as any sister in the world ever could, thanked God with me for this enormous victory. These women had worked hard for me, saved my bacon more times than I could count, but I'd never loved or appreciated them more than I did that night.

Kristal ignored our blubbering. She ate that entire shrimp, then started in on the next. When she finished all six of them, she asked for a bite of my salad. She ordered one of her own—with Italian dressing. Then she finished off my steak with asparagus and crab.

In spite of my thankfulness, I was concerned. I'd always heard it was dangerous to break a fast—even a three day fast—with anything but fruit juice or something very bland. This kid of mine had not had one single thing in her stomach for more than three months! And she had broken her fast with shrimp and cocktail sauce, Italian dressing and steak, for Heaven's sake! I worried about her blowing up or something. But I had been too overjoyed that she was actually eating to stop her.

In the end, nothing happened. Nothing got stuck, nothing stopped up, nothing hurt. Her stomach was just fine the next day. I casually asked if she wanted pancakes with Jeff and I. She ate three pancakes for breakfast and went back to eating a regular diet after that. Incredible.

In retrospect, I think that she just got used to not eating. She hadn't been able to eat while she was sick, then even when she was better, she couldn't bring herself to begin again. It seemed like a version of anorexia (though this was before I'd ever heard the word). I give God the credit for breaking that association in her head. This, too, like so many other things in my life, I can only attribute to His marvelous mercy and grace.

The food helped immediately. Kristal got stronger, gained about 15 pounds and went back to school by the end of January. She loved being back with her friends, hanging out and having fun. She finally got her wish. She was a normal kid again.

Finally!

About March Kristal and her friends started thinking about the next big thing on their list—the Junior Prom. One day she came home from the mall to report that she'd found the perfect prom dress. No boyfriend, no date, mind you, just the dress. We went out to look at it.

Kristal tried it on and glided out of the dressing room to show me. The dress was satin in a gorgeous pale shade of peach. An inch-deep ruffle around the not-too-low-cut neckline, fitted at the waist. It was floor length with peach lace peeking out from under the hem.

"Oh, honey, it's beautiful. No doubt about that. And it's not as expensive as I thought it'd be. But are you sure you're going to the prom?"

"Oh, I'm going all right," she said, glowing as she stared at her reflection. "If no one asks me, I'll just ask them. Even if I have to go with the girls, I'm going to the prom."

"Well then, Kiddo, I think you're going to need that dress. It really does look great on you."

On an unusually hot Sunday afternoon that spring, Kristal and I went looking for a new car. At the Subaru dealership, we picked out a very cool white station wagon with black trim along the sides and a roof rack. It had air conditioning—a feature I would not have thought I needed on a cooler day. Then the haggling began.

Car shopping is not like regular shopping. For one thing, there's no bargain rack, which is the only logical spot to begin any shopping expedition. There are no price tags. Did we want undercoating? An extended warranty? How much was the van worth? I had bought cars before and knew what to expect, but I hadn't thought to fill Kristal in on the process. This haggling was driving Kristal crazy. Twice she had stomped out to sit in the van.

"Why does the price keep changing?" she asked when the salesman went to talk to the boss. "Why don't they get their act together and just give us a price? It seems like they're trying to rip us off."

"It's our job not to let them do that. I know it's dumb, but this is the game that car dealerships play. Just hang in there. He'll be back with a new price in a minute."

After two hours of back and forth offers, we agreed on a trade-in price for the van, but we got hung up on one point. They wanted me to put up $1,000 cash in addition to several thousand dollars worth of equity in the van. I said no and got up to walk away when the salesman suggested that we take the car and drive some place to sit and think about it.

So, as blindly as an alligator climbs into a trap after a raw chicken, we climbed into the shiny new Subaru, cranked up the air conditioning, and headed for a nearby park. With that new car sparkling and shining in the parking lot, Kristal and I sat on the grass and prayed. The $1,000 was a real sticking point. I couldn't make myself agree to that and didn't have $1,000 to give them anyway. Suddenly, Kristal spoke up.

"I feel like they'll just take away that $1,000."

"What?" I said, blowing all the air out of my lungs. "Are you nuts? What will they do with $1000? They can't just add it into the purchase price at this point. After all that haggling we already did, they won't just drop the price by $1000! THAT would be a miracle!"

"Well," she said, shaking her head as if she were very sure of herself, "maybe this will be a miracle. If this is God, I think that $1,000 will just go away."

This kid cracks me up, I thought, but you gotta love her faith. We climbed back into the Subaru and drove back to the dealership, laughing all the way at the ridiculous thought. When we arrived, I didn't say a word. I just handed the salesman the keys and shook my head. He didn't stay silent, however.

"Well," he began, "you're not going to believe this. In fact, I don't believe this, but the boss has dropped that requirement for $1,000. He NEVER does this."

"What?" I said, stunned. Kristal stood beside me, hands folded over her chest and grinning like a Chesire cat.

"It's late and we haven't sold a single car all day. He can't let that happen, so he just dropped the $1,000. Ready to sign the papers?"

We drove home in our brand new, cool, new-car-smelling Subaru, praising God all the way.

15
MOM MIRACLE

I always thought of myself as a huge disappointment to my mother. Mom was a South Dakota girl who was cooking enormous meals for farm crews by the time she was 12. In this environment, everyone in her German/Dutch family worked hard—with the possible exception of my grandmother, who as a diabetic, had special dispensation.

I remember a couple of things about visiting my grandparents' farm as a child. The incredible softness of the baby rabbits Grandpa raised. Licking spoonfuls of freshly churned butter like it was ice cream. The time my grandpa's teeth flew all the way across the room when he sneezed. The chicken who ran up a tree and out on a limb, squirting blood all the way, after Grandpa had chopped his head off on a stump. There were a lot of surprises on the farm.

But one thing you could count on in my family was the food. Boy, could my mother cook. Everyday dinners were good, but she was renowned for her cinnamon rolls and the delectable crescent-shaped rolls she called butter horns. From morning until after 11 at night, my mom worked. Unfortunately for us, she didn't like to work alone, and expected everyone in the house to work right along with her.

Ours was not a house of Saturday morning cartoons. Saturday was work day, and it began WAY too early. We changed all the bedding, washed all the clothes, scrubbed or vacuumed all the floors, dusted the whole house. And that was before lunch. No excuses, no arguments, no letup. My mother's favorite saying was, "Children are to be seen but not heard." When I went over to a friends' houses and heard mothers chatting with them as if they were real people, I was amazed. My mother and I didn't chat. Ever.

And as the oldest daughter, I was most responsible. I was an example for my younger sisters, my mother often reminded me. If I slacked off or got sidetracked reading a book or making doll clothes or whatever, she screamed. Usually something to the effect of, "You are the laziest person I've ever seen! You're going to end up just like your Aunt Lillian," as if that was the worst fate ever.

Aunt Lillian was my mom's younger sister, but you'd never know they were raised by the same parents. Apparently, she got the afternoon-nap genes; my mom got the no-end-to-the-work genes. Lillian had four kids we really liked but every time we went to her house, we had to step over the clothes and dishes and stuff that covered every surface. Lillian was a friendly, loving, laid-back lady. She seemed to collect many things all at once but didn't adhere to the "a place for everything and everything in its place" method of housekeeping that my mom preached. And at 5'1" she weighed about 300 soft, squishy pounds. Growing up to be like Aunt Lillian was an enormous threat.

When I was 12, several things changed for me. That was the year that Boeing laid off thousands and thousands of men, including my dad. With the work force far exceeding available jobs in Seattle, Dad could find only occasional, sporadic work, often loading trucks on the evening shift.

Because of that, Mom went to work at a local variety store called Chubby and Tubby. I became the housewife. I had little sisters to watch, floors to vacuum, and a dinner to get on the table every day. And it had all better be done when Mom got home.

But that was only one of my changes. I still wasn't allowed to speak freely and would never think to confide anything in my mother. After seeing that I needed a bra, a neighbor included one in a hand-me-down basket from her daughter. I wore it through my entire seventh grade year. My mother never noticed.

The one person who did notice my budding figure was Uncle Art, my dad's brother. As a truck driver, he happened through Seattle every couple of years. When dad sent me up to wake him for dinner one day, he made me lay down on the bed beside him, then stuck his hand up my shirt. My mouth refused to open, but in my head I screamed. Fortunately, Dad called again and I got out of there before things went any further. But that three minutes still affects me.

My mother had always warned, "It hurts to be beautiful"—usually while ramming bobby pins into our heads on Saturday night. So, when my uncle was running his grimy, callused fingers over me, I figured this was just more of what she meant. If you have boobs or are pretty, men will hurt you, I concluded.

But I couldn't talk about any of this stuff that was exploding in my head—especially to my mom. No one knew my pain. I didn't trust anyone with what was going on in my head, not even my best friend. The only friend, the only thing, available was food. I had always been a skinny kid, but suddenly that changed.

That was when the "just like Aunt Lillian" threats escalated. "Take that!" I'd whisper, while chomping down on a cookie, in another room of course, at the same nano-second that my mom was yelling at me not to have a cookie. My eating was one thing she couldn't control. With the dimes a neighbor paid me for doing her ironing, I began sending my little sister to the store to buy me candy bars.

My older brother was going through changes too. He'd been angry since he was a toddler, but since he wasn't allowed to speak either, I had no idea what was going on with him. He took on a morning paper route. Afternoons, he often smacked us around, beat us up. Sometimes Lorraine, the ironing neighbor, came over to try to break it up, but as helpful as she tried to be, I couldn't tell her the truth either.

So I ate. Most times when I took a bite, it was as if I was biting my mom or at least her control of me. It was an act of rebellion against her, against all of the adults I couldn't trust. I was angry and hurt.

And as nice as my dad was, I was mad at him too. He hadn't protected me—from his brother, my brother or my mom. Instead of stepping in when she was berating us, he shook his head and walked away, the same thing he did when she berated him. He was too nice for his own good. And mine.

So, I became chunky. Just like Aunt Lillian. I didn't get anywhere near 300 pounds, but what is that they say about self-fulfilling prophecies? Anyway, I felt like an unlovable failure, and knew nothing I could do would make my mother love me.

That April, my parents invited Kristal and Jeff to spend their spring break with them in Arizona. I couldn't go because I was committed to help with a women's retreat that weekend. Kristal was stronger than she'd been for some time, still in remission and I knew she'd take care of Jeff on the plane. So, they flew off to Arizona while I attended a weekend women's retreat.

During one session, the speaker asked us to recall a time of peace in our lives—like the time our mothers had read us stories or pushed us on the swing. But as hard as I tried, I couldn't think of a single time I had sat on my mother's lap. Not one. I did remember calling to my mom repeatedly to come and push me on the swing at Melgaard Park, but she was always busy catching up with her friends.

It was hard raising four kids, I tried to rationalize. But it didn't work. I had uncovered a well of anger a hundred feet deep. No wonder it echoed so loudly in my life. And that anger was all directed at my mother.

When this kind of hurt had come to my attention in the past, God had somehow cauterized the wound and allowed me to forgive. This time, however, that didn't happen. Sunday morning, I returned home more furious than ever at my mother. I didn't understand, didn't know how I'd ever get over this.

I picked up the kids at the airport Sunday night and they chattered all the way home. Jeff had followed my dad around, playing with all his tools and truck stuff. Kristal had spent the whole time with my mom. They had toured Arizona, seen the Grand Canyon and even a few sights in Mexico in the motor home.

I knew I should call to thank my parents, but I was still too angry at mom to speak to her, so I put it off. After Kristal left for school Tuesday morning, I called and was relieved when Dad answered the phone. He said Mom was still sleeping, something she could do now that they were retired. We chatted for about 15 minutes, then I thanked him profusely for being so good to the kids and we hung up.

But just after I got Jeff to the bus, Dad called back.

"After we talked I went in to wake your mom," he began slowly. "But she didn't answer. So I went around the other side of the bed and shook her. She was cold."

Cold? What do you mean cold? Stunned, I didn't say a word. My mind reeled.

"The paramedics have been here," Dad said quietly, weeping as he talked. "She's gone, Shirl. I can't believe it either. They said it was arteriosclerosis. I need you to call the other kids."

How could this be? She was only 58! No one dies in their sleep at 58! And the kids had just spent a week shopping, visiting Mexico, traveling through the desert with her. She'd been fine. Just fine.

My mom was gone. I would never be able to talk to her again. Never have to talk to her again. Never have to disappoint her again. Oh, I cried of course, I always cry. But why didn't it hurt more? Wasn't I supposed to be in incredible pain?

I decided not to disturb the kids at school but to wait until they came home. But in the afternoon, Kristal called to ask if she could go to her friend Deanna's. I asked her to come home instead.

"But I haven't seen my friends all week. We need to catch up."

"I really need you to come home."

"Why?" she asked, suddenly serious. "Something's wrong, isn't it?"

"Just come home, Honey. We need to talk."

"What's wrong?" She paused, then said, "Grandma's dead, isn't she?"

I nearly dropped the phone. How does she KNOW this stuff? I didn't say a word. Didn't want to tell her on the phone. "Just come home please," I whispered.

"I'll be right there," she said.

When she got home, we cried. She told me about all the time she and my mom had spent together, the shopping, the laughs they'd had.

"But when I waved goodbye to her," she said, "I knew I'd never see her again."

"What??? How can that be? How did you know?"

"I can't explain it. Maybe it was God. But a feeling came over me, and I just knew it would be the last time I ever saw her."

I told her what I had experienced over the weekend and admitted that I didn't know what to do about it. I wondered aloud how I would ever get past this pain and forgive my mom.

"Wait here," she said suddenly, then ran for her bedroom. I sat there, stunned, shaking my head, the way I often did when I hung out with my incredible daughter/best friend.

Kristal returned a minute later and shoved a softly wrapped package at me—an early birthday present for me from my mom. Inside were two things my mother had embroidered. One was a hand-stitched 18-inch square of white linen with a floral border in black, red and green thread. The center said, "May all the love you give away return to you every day." The other said, "Bless this day our daily bread" in slate blue. They were beautiful, but not as beautiful as the story Kristal told me.

"Grandma worked on these the whole time we were there," she said, fingering the delicate flowers. "While we were driving in the motor home or watching TV, she kept this in her lap—always stitching on it. She kept taking stitches out to redo them. She said she wanted them to be perfect for you. She kept telling me how proud she was of you, how much she loved you."

I bawled like a baby. And with every tear, forgiveness flowed. Kristal and I held each other for a long time. She kept telling me stories my mom had told her about when I was a kid. Amazing. By the time we finished, nearly every drop in my deep well of anger was gone. The bitterness had evaporated like a little puddle in the tropical sun.

The beauty of it for me was that my daughter had gotten to tell me that my mother loved me. I can't imagine my mother ever telling me those things, but she was able to share them with Kristal. It made me appreciate God all the more for the creative way He handled this, blessing all three generations at once.

And I kept thinking about the timing. If Mom had died a week earlier, my kids would have missed the chance to tuck away great memories of their grandmother. And if she had died while the kids were there, they would have been devastated. I can't imagine how Dad would have coped with all the details when he had them to worry about. And God's timing, I decided, was perfect.

But then...

Three days after Mom's funeral, Kristal had one of her monthly checkups. As always, doctors tested her blood for those pesky leukemia cells, then let me look at the slide too. Red blood cells are identically red; the white ones looked like little round jellyfish. But under the microscope, that wasn't all I saw. Though I had never seen a leukemia cell, I knew. It was back.

In this one tiny dot of Kristal's blood, some cells had legs and arms and strangely shaped other appendages. Some were ten times as large as a normal blood cell. They were purple, they were dark, they looked evil. This evil was eating my daughter alive. Those were the cells that stole all the nutrition, starving the red blood cells that provide energy and the white ones that fight infection.

This was Kristal's third relapse. I knew that each time this insidious disease returned, her chances of survival slid down an ever-steeper slope. My knees buckled. Tears streamed down my face. I couldn't breathe. I thought back to God's promise never to give us more than we can handle, but I honestly didn't know how I would handle any more.

But Kristal was not surprised. How did she always KNOW these things? I thought back to one of the questions she had asked when we were deciding whether she and Jeff could go visit Grandma and Grandpa.

"If you knew something was wrong, would you still let me go?" she'd asked. She had known then. That could have been the first time I asked myself how I was going to go on without this child I loved so dearly. But as soon as the thought popped into my head, I shoved it out like a mama bird shoves her ready-to-fly little one out of the nest. I refused to believe that God was going to allow this to happen to her or to me.

It felt more like she was holding me than I was holding her. Our faith was strong but this was a mighty blow. They started chemo immediately. At first it was effective, but within a couple of weeks, her counts started to rise. Kristal was not surprised about that either.

Now the leukemia was back again. Especially this time, Kristal didn't want anyone feeling sorry for her. She insisted that she not be treated as a sick person. Friends rarely stopped by and when they did, she felt their pity. She wouldn't allow anyone in her hospital room with a negative attitude. She asked me to put up a sign that said NO TEARS. IF YOU CAN'T SMILE, YOU CAN'T COME IN.

She was ready to be with Jesus a long time before I was ready to let her go.

My dad didn't leave the Seattle area immediately after Mom's funeral. He wasn't ready to return to Arizona alone so he offered to stick around and help us, which kept his mind off his own grief. He was terrific and flexible, getting Jeff off to school or staying with Kristal while I was at work.

We went back to the insurance company to see if they might change their mind about paying for a bone marrow transplant. Doctors now thought it was her only hope. In fact, when Kristal was first diagnosed, Dr. Dan had suggested that Gary and I consider getting together and having another baby in case it came to this. I thought he was kidding and never mentioned it to Gary. A dozen years after a divorce? I didn't think so. Now I wished I'd at least discussed it with him.

Anyway, in the beginning of Kristal's illness, bone marrow transplantation was a cutting edge procedure and the insurance company had refused to pay for it. Doctors had been making progress in combating leukemia in the last couple of years, but the procedure was still considered experimental.

"There are seven markers in the blood," Dr. Dan explained. "Five of the markers need to match to even give her a chance."

Even though the insurance hadn't agreed to cover the estimated $500,000 the procedure cost, Kristal's aunts, uncles and cousins all came in to be tested. The procedure didn't require much heroism—all it took was a simple blood sample. We all waited a week or so for the results to come in, but in the end, no one qualified anyway. No one, not even me or her dad, had more than three matching markers. They checked the national bone marrow registry, but not one single soul registered in all of the United States had enough of the markers required to save my daughter's life. It made me wonder how anyone in the world can believe in evolution.

Anyone who has ever been tested is listed in the National Bone Marrow Registry. To this day, one of my biggest hopes is that one day I have the opportunity to donate marrow to save someone's life. I wish someone had been there to say yes for Kristal.

16
JUNIOR PROM

As if all this weren't enough, I had promised long before to produce a Mother's Day Fashion Show at a local church's Mother-Daughter Tea. Kristal insisted that I not back out. So, against my better judgment, I set about fitting 25 kids into outfits both they and their mothers loved—not an easy task—while gathering accessories to highlight them. Since I also emceed this part of the program, I had to write the commentary on every outfit. All this took many hours that I would rather have spent at the hospital with Kristal.

So, on the day before Mother's Day I stood at the podium with the teddy bear that always accompanied me to such events. As I looked out at the mothers, daughters and granddaughters before me, I was totally unprepared for the depth of emotion that came over me. All dressed in their finest attire, they gathered expectantly at perfectly laid tables. I struggled to read the unimportant fashion commentary.

Instead, I wanted to blurt out that my mother just died very suddenly in the night and my daughter isn't expected to live out the month.

Nearly choking on the rhetoric before me, I wanted to tell them—scream at them—to treasure their precious relationships. I wanted to order them to apologize for every stupid thing they had ever done or said to each other, to forgive the trivial things that stood in the way of open, healthy family ties. I wanted to warn them that life doesn't go on forever, to encourage them to make the best of every day.

But this wasn't the time or place. I held my tongue and cried silently through the remainder of the luncheon, then slipped out to head back to the hospital.

I had been so busy with Kristal that poor Jeff had taken a back seat. I didn't realize how badly he suffered until I got the Mother's Day card the teacher had the first graders make. He'd written me a poem. I can only quote the last line that said, "Never has time to play with me." It broke my heart. I hadn't given him enough credit or enough time. Hadn't thought he was old enough to know better. Now I could only hold him and apologize and try to explain but I don't think he got it. Even though I saw no sign of things letting up, I vowed to be a better mother to my precious son.

Unless people asked about Kristal's illness, I didn't generally bring it up. It seemed that many people, usually moms, wanted to hear what was going on with her. If I hadn't seen friends for a while or I ran into customers at the grocery store, they usually asked about Kristal's latest hospital visit or blood test or whatever. Normally, they kept asking, kept wanting to hear everything that had happened since the last time I'd seen them—the chemotherapy, the fevers, the hair loss, the vomiting, or the latest horror.

Don't get me wrong. It was wonderful that so many people cared. But in order to tell the story I'd have to relive it, to feel every sorrow and pain and heartache all over again. My friend would sympathize and shake her head and say how horrible it was, then walk away. She could go home and fix dinner for her healthy family.

I couldn't do that.

When I'd finished updating them, especially if they wanted all the gory details, I often felt like my guts were laying there in a pile, spilt out on Aisle 7, right in front of the spaghetti sauce and crushed tomatoes. I felt exposed. Vulnerable. Sad. This sometimes happened five or six times a day. The constant retelling of it was exhausting.

People's reactions often surprised me too. After hearing of the latest battle, they often said, "You're so brave," or "I don't think I could do that" or "I admire your faith."

That killed me. If they had only seen me curled in a fetal position or held by my seat belt hours earlier, I'd think. If only they had been sitting in the back row of the hospital chapel in the middle of the night, watching me weep and complain and cry out to God. If only they knew that my wicked heart sometimes wished it was their kid and not mine who was sick.

Cancer is not a battle anyone chooses. We were victims, not volunteers. No one signs up for this. We are not brave; we're just trying to survive. Why don't people understand that? We were all shoved onto this battlefield kicking and screaming. Even if we are driven to our knees or just hanging on to sanity by the tiniest of prayers, people admire us and call us brave. Reaching over to lend a hand seems way more courageous to me.

Fortunately, I had many friends who did just that. One such person was Esther, a woman I hardly knew from the Fox Island Alliance Church. Dressed in heels and a chic gray suit that matched her hair, this tall woman with great posture stopped me in church one morning to say that she'd like to begin praying for Kristal.

Like a project, I thought, groaning inwardly.

"Would it be okay if I started coming by the hospital sometimes?" she asked. "I don't want to intrude on your family time. I just intend to pray for her. I'll sit over in the corner or someplace out of the way. I don't expect you to entertain me or even to talk to me if you don't feel like it."

Why would I say no? We can all use prayer, right?

So, Esther began showing up at the hospital, always in a classy dress or suit and heels. She'd wander in and sit in the corner. Daytimes usually, but often at night too. A few times she even stayed until after midnight. At first, it was strange to have this woman we didn't know muttering to herself in the corner. But Esther kept coming and we got to know her. Sometimes she played Connect Four with us or watched a movie. Once she showed up at dinnertime with an elegant presentation of asparagus tips, black olives, carrot sticks, ham rolls, cheeses, fresh bread and sparkling cider. Just dropped it off and left, wouldn't even eat with us.

Esther was full of surprises. She and Kristal became great friends. It was an unlikely paring—this 65-year-old and 16-year-old—and I never did understand what Esther got out of the relationship. Maybe the feeling of being a hero for a short time was all she needed. For whatever reason, I sometimes arrived to find them laughing like girlfriends. Then one day Kristal excitedly showed me the jewelry Esther was lending her to wear to the Junior Prom.

"Esther brought in a big, wooden jewelry box this high," Kristal said, extending her hand about three feet above her bed, "with about a dozen drawers. We had such fun! She told me about each piece of jewelry and where she had worn it or where she got it, then she said I could choose whatever I wanted to wear to the prom! Aren't these gorgeous? And they're REAL!"

Flipping her hands and head around so they caught the light, she modeled a pearl and diamond bracelet, and a ruby and diamond necklace and earring set. I hardly knew Esther, yet she had become such a wonderful friend to my daughter who so needed someone to talk to. She was like an angel. And how brave of her to step so close to a life that was so fragile.

Esther left as mysteriously as she arrived. Some years later, her husband was accused of a crime and I spent days in the courtroom with her, praying quietly in the corner.

Anyway, Kristal wasn't going to school, wasn't hanging

out with her friends, wasn't dating anyone, yet it was vital to her that she go to the prom in May. So, a friend named Doug offered to take her. The prom was set for Saturday, but she'd been in the hospital for weeks and doctors weren't making any promises. No one knew if she'd be strong enough to go. Again, the chemo had made her weak as a kitten—the-runt-of-the-litter-kitten.

But the day before the prom, Kristal passed their blood tests, so my dad and I loaded her up and took her home from the hospital. She was ecstatic.

Just as any girl getting ready for prom, she bustled around the house getting ready. She spiked up her two inches of hair. My trained eye could still spot the IV line under her peach satin dress, but with blush to hide her palor, some mascara, and Esther's jewels, she positively glowed.

After two rolls of film, I got a great shot that reflects the flash behind her in the bathroom mirror. By then, me and my camera were getting on Kristal's nerves. Big time. When Doug rang the doorbell, Kristal was still in the bathroom. As she hustled to the door, I elbowed in and whispered, "Wait, wait!" You know—so I could get a good shot as she opened the door.

She flipped around at me like a Ninja fighter and shot me a look I couldn't mistake. "Back off!" her big brown eyes shouted, loud and clear.

"Okay, okay!" I said, hands up in surrender. I got out of the way.

She and Doug looked wonderful together and my dad and I both cried when they left. Then we sat down to wait. Kristal had already been up getting ready for hours. It was more time than she'd been on her feet for weeks. Doug was considerate enough to say that he'd bring her home whenever she was ready. Dad and I were betting how long she'd last at the prom—Dad had 9, I had 10.

So, at 10 we started expecting her. At 11, we began

to get a little worried. Midnight came and went. One, then two. We were getting frantic. Kristal couldn't possibly still be on her feet at this hour! And yet, when she did get home, she positively floated in the door. Her smile filled every pore on her face. I was relieved and thrilled because I hadn't seen that for a long, long time. She absolutely glowed with excitement.

"Doug was perfect!" she gushed. "He let me set the pace. He's a senior, you know, so he knew a lot of people there too. But I didn't just hang out with him all night. I talked to tons of people I haven't seen for months...

"Everyone was surprised to see me and it was sooo good to catch up... Deanna, Kerry, Trinna, Carey and I had our picture taken together—without our dates. I can't wait to see how it comes out...

"Mrs. Schultz said this was my night—like the prom was just for me. I had such a good time, Mom! Thanks for not making me be home at 10 or something..."

Kristal kept chatting as I helped her get ready for bed. I think she dozed off in the middle of a story. But by the next morning everything had changed. It was as if she'd used every ounce of strength at the prom. Kristal was so exhausted that she couldn't get out of bed. Her face had broken out and she was pale as buttermilk again. Just as she'd been in the beginning of this dreaded disease.

A few days later, just as I was waking up in the morning, in that moment just before my eyes opened when I prayed for Kristal, I saw that peach satin prom dress again. Not the whole thing—my view was just a slice. I could only see the skirt from below the waist to the lace that peeked out from the bottom of the hem.

The dress was swaying to soft music and I could see a horizontal slice of Kristal dancing. Then when she turned, I saw her partner. He wore the most shimmering white robe I had ever seen. They moved as one, gracefully and perfectly, this incredible, soft glowing robe and the peach satin. And suddenly, way under the surface of my thoughts, I knew.

God was showing me that my daughter would soon dance with Jesus. I knew I would bury her in her prom dress.

Aauuuugh. A dull pain filled my soul and shriveled me from the inside out. I curled around it.

But I couldn't think about it. Couldn't believe it. Refused to believe it. Quickly, before I had even opened my eyes to look at the thought in the daylight, I tucked it deep into a hidden pocket in my mind and forgot about it.

I never told Kristal. I didn't want her to give up.

I didn't have anyone to tell. My friends were long gone. This disease was all-consuming for both of us. I still saw friends at church or in the grocery store, but never had time to chat over coffee or go to the movies. With the possible exception of Joan at the hospital who knew exactly what was happening, there was no one with whom I could sit down and talk. It was a wonderful/awful time.

About this time, Kristal decided she wanted to see the ocean. So, my dad, who was still trying to find his place in the world after Mom's death, flew to Arizona to pick up his motor home so he could fulfill her last wish—to take her camping. But by the time he returned a few days later, she was too weak and couldn't go. Dad parked his motor home in our giant carport and stayed to help Jeff and me handle things.

Within the week, Kristal was back in the hospital. They gave her antibiotics to kill the infections that plagued her. Did everything they could to make her comfortable. But nothing really made her comfortable.

And I kept thinking about what my friend Donna had said back when Kristal first went into remission and refused treatment.

"What are you trying to do, kill her?" she had asked.

I tried to put it out of my mind, but the line popped to the surface pretty regularly. Was her pain my fault? Kristal and I had argued for a week about the decision to continue with treatment after her first remission. Could I have tied her to the bed? Forced her to take the chemo? If I had insisted, would she be facing this now? Was I killing her? It killed me to think about it. Just in case she had been right, I avoided Donna.

We were back to the daily hospital routine. Dad was spending more time at home with Jeff, I was back to living on the hospital futon. Each day Kristal got weaker. She couldn't walk down the halls with me and her IV anymore. Then she couldn't stand. The only time she got out of bed anymore was to travel six feet to the bathroom—and that required my help. By the time she returned to her bed she was ready for a nap.

When she nodded off, especially at night, I headed for the hospital chapel. In the close, consecrated quiet of that little room, I felt safe. Almost hugged. I could talk to the Lord, scream at Him, beg Him to spare my daughter. I could read His word and remember His promises. I could be honest about my pain and anger, knowing He'd never be mad. I could cry all I needed to cry and no one would pity me or be afraid to speak to me.

Somehow, when I walked out the door of that tiny room I always felt 90 percent better than I had when I'd arrived.

I knew He understood. The God of the universe understood my pain. In fact, He was the only one I knew who had been through the same thing. As His only Son suffered and hung on the cross—for me and all of my miserable sins, God Himself must have felt the very same way.

This Christianity thing kept unfolding—showing me great rewards I had not even thought to expect. It was internal. It was external. It was eternal. Go figure.

When a friend had invited me to join Bible Study Fellowship two years earlier, I decided to try it. I knew it meant reading the Bible and answering homework questions every day and listening to a lecture every week. I'd made it a priority and for much of this year and last, I'd been curled up in a hospital chair studying, but I'd learned much about God and gotten to know many new people too.

The old hymns we sang each Thursday weren't my favorites, but before we sang, our leader, Caroline, always said, "Please stand with me…"

That became my theme for this year. Each week, many of these 300 women—young mothers with toddlers in tow, single career women in suits and experienced grandmothers—asked what was happening with Kristal and how they could pray for her.

At the end of the season, there was one special day when we were supposed to share with the others what this class had meant to us. I didn't often speak in public, but my heart beat until I thought it would break through my rib cage and I knew I had to thank these wonderful friends who had cared and prayed for us all year.

I knew it was God promting me to get up and saying something. Finally, I stood.

"My favorite part of the week," I began, "is when Caroline says, 'Please stand with me.' Because that's what I feel—that you stand with me. That you have stood with me all year. Most of you know that my daughter has been fighting leukemia. This year I've also gone through a divorce and my mother died, so it's been a tough year.

"But I know that every single one of you are standing WITH me in whatever I'm going through.

"Some of you have stood FOR me when I was too weak to stand alone.

"And I know that if I get out of line, you'll also stand

up TO me and straighten me out. You have cared about me as if we were family. I am so thankful."

And when I sat down, as scary as it had been to address this big crowd, I felt as safe as a little tree in the center of a big forest.

17

THE WAYWARD TEARDROP

While she was in the hospital, Kristal heard a rumor that someone in her class had tried to commit suicide.

"I can't BELIEVE she'd do that!" she cried. "Doesn't she KNOW how valuable life is? Every day I try SO hard to live and she wants to throw it all away!! How could she even THINK about that? Doesn't she KNOW how much that would hurt her family?"

"Of course she doesn't. People in pain aren't usually thinking about other people at all. Honey, you don't know what her life is like, no idea what she faces when she walks in her own front door every day. She must have had her reasons."

"But she has no idea what she's throwing away or she wouldn't be doing it. Maybe I could go tell her. Shoot, I'll tell the whole school! Maybe I'll get a degree and talk to teenagers everywhere about the value of life. About how God says He created us all in our mother's wombs and He has a plan for our lives. That we are all precious in His sight…"

I recently ran across all those verses underlined in Kristal's Bible. The same way she underlined Psalm 45:9-11 that begins, "'Oh God, my Rock,' I cry, 'why have you forsaken me? Why must I suffer these attacks from my enemies?' and ends with 'For I know that I shall have plenty of reasons to praise him for all he will do. He is my help! He is my God.'"

There are at least a dozen others. Most of them are about struggling. Overcoming. One said, "Spare me, Lord! Let me recover and be filled with happiness again before my death."

I know now that my daughter suffered much more than she let on. On the surface, she was handling this disease well. She refused to talk about the fact that it might steal her very life. We tried very hard to protect each other by talking of positive things, happy outcomes. Kristal rarely mentioned her misery to me, but she knew how seriously ill she was.

In fact, I think now that the Lord told her she would not survive. Another verse she underlined was 2 Kings 20:1, "Hezekiah now became deathly sick, and Isaiah the prophet went to visit him. 'Set your affairs in order and prepare to die,' Isaiah told him. The Lord says you won't recover.'"

Even when her friends visited, she asked them what was going on with them—wouldn't tell them about her struggles. She just wanted to be a normal kid. She didn't want anyone crying in her presence—even me. That was hard. I still had the slow leak that refused to be controlled.

After all this time spent together in trying circumstances, Kristal and I had become best friends. With a couple of exceptions, friends of her own age had stopped visiting. Jennifer remembers reading her Psalms during her bad days but mostly, her friends talked about boyfriends and learning to drive. It was too hard not to get depressed about her sickness, too hard to think of some middle-of-the-road thing to say.

My friends helped when they could, but they had their own families, their own troubles. After all, this had been going on for almost two years. Jeff was with us when he wasn't in school or at his dad's, but for most of every day, every week, every month, Kristal and I were alone together.

We talked about everything. She made it clear that she didn't want anyone coming "to look at me" in a coffin, but wanted to be buried first, then have a service, "if you have to."

"Where do you want to be buried?" I asked.

"Well, I don't know. Where do YOU want to be buried?"

"I can't imagine leaving Fox Island, so I guess I'd say there. You've seen the little cemetery there, right? It always looks so peaceful with the rhododendrons and the big shade trees."

"Yeah, I've even seen deer there. I guess that'd be good."

"Okay, well, IF we need to buy a spot there, then we will. But I'm not buying any real estate until we need it."

"Deal. Fox Island it is."

Kristal and I were close in ways I have never been close to anyone—talking about the hard things, the awful, unfair things in life and the glory of the Lord in the midst of it all. She was ready to die, ready to end the pain, ready to be with Jesus.

My sister Rhonda was in town for the weekend and offered to spend the night in the hospital with Kristal so I could sleep in my own bed. We planned to meet at church on Sunday morning. Jeff and I arrived and sat in our usual spot near the front. But the service wasn't starting on time, which was unusual. Then there seemed to be a commotion in the foyer. One of the ushers came in and called me to join them. Rhonda was in tears in the lobby, surrounded by Pastor Andy and a couple of other friends.

"One of the nurses told me Kristal probably wouldn't make it through the day," Rhonda said haltingly.

I let out a big sigh.

"Yeah, yeah," I replied, pulling her toward the sanctuary. "I've heard that before. Dry your tears. We need to go praise the Lord. She'll be fine until we get there."

Mouths flew open all around the small crowd that

had gathered to feel sorry for me. In retrospect, it does sound callous. But those people had never heard that before. I had. Numerous times. About Clayton, Eddie, Kristal and others we had known. I think it was a tool the staff used to prepare people for the worst. But they weren't usually right and somehow I knew they wouldn't be right that day either.

For a long time now, my life had been feeling like a helium balloon, bobbing and weaving like it was tied to an antenna in a used car lot. I knew I needed to tether myself to the living God, to anchor my soul. In order to live through these days myself, I needed an hour to hang onto His coattails for all I was worth. And I just knew God would not take Kristal while I was praising Him.

So, with Rhonda in tow, I marched back into the sanctuary and the service finally started. The pastor asked our 75-member church family to pray for Kristal because she was close to death. People shook their heads in shock, not believing that this could truly be happening.

When the praise music began, I raised my hands in surrender to my Lord, knowing He was in control. He knew what He was doing, I didn't. I knew that the only way to hang on to my sanity was to look up, to keep my eyes on Jesus. Tears streamed down my face, but my soul was filled with peace. He had proven over and over that He would take care of us all, whether Kristal lived or died. I trusted Him with the future of my family.

After the service, Rhonda and Jeff headed one way and I headed for the hospital. Kristal did look worse than I'd ever seen her. She had been through so much. Her Grandma Hennie had watched her handle the chemo, watched her keep up her spirits and watched her not complain about any of it. She had nicknamed Kristal, True Grit.

Now her bones, which were producing hundreds of thousands of leukemia cells each day, ached with the intense pressure. Kristal's spleen was trying so hard to flush them from her system that her stomach was distended, making her look like a starving child in a National Geographic magazine. But the worst thing was that she hadn't showered for days and her hair stuck up in greasy spikes all over her head.

"You'd feel better if you got cleaned up, you know," I said. "Want me to help you?"

"Wish they had a tub. I can't stand up for a shower."

The hospital did have a bathtub, a nice deep one. I ran off to ask the nurses to prepare it for her. Just rolling over in bed seemed to exhaust her these days. She needed the wheelchair to get a few doors down the hall. While she relaxed in the hot, scented water, I gently shampooed what was left of her hair.

"Rhonda panicked this morning," I finally told her. "Susan told her she didn't think you'd make it through the day."

"Really? I don't feel THAT bad," she said with a little chuckle. "Do you think it's that close?"

How does a mother answer a question like that? I didn't want Kristal to give up, didn't want her to think I'd given up. And I still held out some small hope that God would send a miracle.

"Heck, no," I said. "I don't think you're going anywhere. And I won't believe it until you breathe your very last breath. But I want to reserve judgment on how bad you look until I see you with clean hair and pajamas."

"I don't want to die in the hospital," Kristal said quietly. "Can we just go home?"

"Oh, Honey, of course we can go home. How about today?"

She simply nodded.

"You relax while the water is hot. I'll go tell the nurses we're leaving."

Kristal did look a whole lot better clean. She held her head high for the first time in days. There was so much she couldn't control in her life right now that I think it gave her a sense of power, a sense of dignity, to be able to decide this one thing.

By the time I'd packed up Mr. Ed and all of our stuff, Dr. Dan had arrived. He'd told me a long time ago that we could do whatever we wanted in the end, including going home if we chose to. Even though it was Sunday, he arranged for a home health care nurse to come by daily. He secretly called the local mortuary to tell them she was on her way. He went over the details about the morphine drips I'd be administering to deal with Kristal's pain.

Then, hands in the pockets of his khaki cords, he stood in the hallway, waiting for Kristal to be wheeled out of the room that had been ours for so long. We shook hands and shared hugs, but we all had a hard time saying goodbye. I felt sorry to put this kind, caring man through this. He knew it would be the last time he'd see her. It's got to be difficult to give up after treating a patient for nearly two years, difficult to send her home knowing you'll never see her again. I hope he didn't feel like he had failed, because we all knew he'd done all he could.

Outside, Kristal raised her nose to the sky and breathed in fresh air for the first time in weeks. It revived her for a minute, but I think she was asleep before we passed Frisko Freeze's big ice cream cone in the sky.

The morphine she was taking for the pain sometimes played funny tricks on her. When we pulled into the garage and I tried to wake her, she asked, "Did we go to the funeral? Is it over?"

"What funeral?" I asked, confused. "You mean Grandma's funeral? That was weeks ago."

Kristal just shook her head, as if doing that could clear the confusion that morphine pulls along behind it like noisy cans behind a newlywed's car.

I gave her as many choices as I could. Her room was downstairs so that wouldn't work, and she didn't want to use my bed or Jeff's either. She chose the living room couch. I'm sure it made her feel more normal to be right in the center of things, watching TV, talking and sleeping. I set up a table beside her for water, tissues and whatever else she needed. Her IV pole blended in with the pole lamp in the corner and she slept most of the day. Much of the time, she was pretty much out of it on morphine.

She would eat only a bite or two of whatever I offered, but she did have some strange cravings. Again with the Orange Crush. In a bottle, not a can.

"I can taste the metal," Kristal said, as snooty as the princess from The Princess and the Pea.

So, back to the store I went. Several stores, in fact. The first four I tried only carried Orange Crush in a can. Finally, I waltzed into the living room and casually plopped it on her bedside table. It was refreshing just to look at it. You could see the bright orange liquid through the clear bottle. Little beads of cold perspiration ran down the sides. But did she take a nice, refreshing swig? Noooooo.

"I think I'll just look at it a while," she said, gazing longingly at the glass bottle. She pulled Mr. Ed up around her chin. "I'll drink it later."

The bottle of Orange Crush sat there for three days. Every few hours I traded it out for a nice cold one and put the warm one back in the fridge.

"No, I just want to look at it," she kept saying. "I'm gonna drink it. Just not right now."

Then she wanted watermelon. Ice cold watermelon. Although it was not even summer yet, I did find a puny one at an enormous price, but she didn't eat that either.

Kristal was sleeping more and more. The morphine still gave her strange dreams. One night she shot up from the couch.

"I saw Rhonda's babies," she said, breathless.

"Rhonda's babies?" I asked, stunned. "Rhonda doesn't

have any babies."

"I know, I know," she said, settling back into her blanket and closing her eyes. "This is just crazy. I keep having these dreams. I hate this morphine."

But was it just a random crazy dream? I couldn't shake the feeling that she was getting glimpses of heaven. Were these children yet to be born? Could Rhonda have had miscarriages or abortions I didn't know about? Had God introduced Kristal to babies who would have been her cousins? Spooky. Or was it just another one of those things that this amazing child just seemed to know?

Those few days were a blender-full of exhaustion, tender moments and dread. I remember changing dressings, adjusting IV medications and morphine drips, and walking Kristal and her IV pole to the bathroom multiple times a day. She leaned on me heavily. Saying she was weak would be like calling Earth a little blue ball. She slept most of the day as Dad, Jeff and I tiptoed around our precious patient.

Jeff's school was winding down for the year and he was upset that I couldn't go watch him at Field Day. He knew Kristal was sick. I had tried to give him some idea of just how sick she was. Of course he was only six. He had no concept that Dad and I were busy keeping Kristal alive and he often felt ignored. Rightly so.

After being up and down all night, Kristal had gone back to sleep early on Thursday morning when I looked out the window and caught a glimpse of the day before me. Although I desperately wanted to crawl back into my own bed, the sun was headed right for me, inching up over the hill, tossing splashes of pinks and oranges and purples over its shoulder. The water reflected all those colors, making them even more brilliant than God made them in the first place. This was one of the reasons I loved living on an island—the way the water intensified the colors in sunsets and sunrises.

My weariness skedaddled. I felt like the Lord had set aside this tiny bit of time for me and I knew what I had to do. I sneaked into Jeff's room and shook his tiny shoulder to wake him.

"Come on," I said when he groaned. "Let's go camping."

He slid out of bed like he was Gumby. I grabbed a sleeping bag from the hall closet and we headed out the back door. He stumbled down to the water with me, his untied tennis shoes tripping in the dewy grass. With the sleeping bag cushioning the cement bulkhead, we lay on our bellies, whispering and giggling, and said a proper hello to the morning.

My heart was full. But I don't think Jeff really got it—the expansive, incredible beauty of the sunrise, my gratefulness for another day with both of my kids, the moments I felt I had to steal to be with my son. Soon enough, we hiked back up to the house to get ready for another day.

We had developed a routine. Luke, calmer now than he'd been as a puppy, permanently curled up at Kristal's feet, like a sentry to protect her. She draped her hand over the edge of the couch so she could stroke his soft ears. Dad took Jeff back and forth to school. We took turns cooking, took shifts staying up with Kristal in the night, reading to her or to ourselves. After school, Jeff preferred playing in the woods with Mike to tiptoeing around the living room.

Kristal's friend Kerry stopped by one night and chatted for a few minutes before Kristal nodded off. Her dad, Gary, drove the hour to see her one afternoon, but only stayed a few minutes. On Friday, Neen stopped by to drop off something from the store, and we talked her into staying for dinner. We ate at the table but kept talking to Kristal, who was in the next room. Poor Neen. What had become normal to us was breaking her heart, and she didn't stay long. She was, of course, used to covering for me at the store, not to spending time on our strange death watch.

Kristal sometimes bolted upright in what I had come to recognize as another morphine-induced glimpse into another world. Luke always jumped up too, anxious to see what was going on.

"Well, did I FINISH?" she practically screamed at me.

"Did you finish what?"

"College!" she said, sounding disgusted that I didn't understand. "Did I finish college?"

"Oh, honey, don't worry about that." I said, smoothing the damp hair from her forehead. "You haven't even finished high school yet. You have plenty of time."

She settled back into her quilt and closed her eyes. Reading to her seemed to calm her, so I picked up my Bible and read from the Psalms. Dad and I spelled each other beside her all night.

Around 5 o'clock Saturday morning, Kristal started having trouble breathing. The leukemia cells had so enlarged her spleen and liver that there was no room for air in her lungs. Since she had decided in the hospital against any emergency procedures, I was surprised when she asked me to call 911 so they could help her breathe.

"But, Kristal," I managed to say, although I could feel my mouth hanging open. "You said you didn't want them here."

"Call 911," she insisted.

"But they'll do the tracheotomy and all that stuff you didn't…"

"What are ya tryin' to do, kill me?" she said, bolting upright.

And at that moment, I probably could have. The little brat! Here I was, dying myself as I watched my beloved child struggle for breath, yet she thought I was trying to kill her! Aaauuugh!

When people die in movies, they usually smile and say something sappy like, "Thanks for the life," or a look of ecstasy appears on their faces immediately before their dramatic exits.

Not Kristal. She fought for every breath. I called Barb, our home health care nurse, who appeared within moments and turned up the morphine. Kristal relaxed and her breathing became easier and increasingly slower.

She closed her eyes. She appeared to be going to back to sleep and began breathing very slowly. I held her close and whispered, "I love you, Kiddo."

Drifting off, she said softly, "I love you too, Mom." Her face was totally peaceful. But just as she breathed her very last breath, she did something that shattered my peace for weeks afterward. One single teardrop sneaked out of her eye and crawled in slow motion down her cheek.

Why would she cry? Kristal never cried. Why a tear just as she is relieved of all her pain? That teardrop occupied my mind for months.

As soon as Dad and I moved away, Luke left his watchful spot. He slowly approached Kristal, sniffed once, then laid his thick head on her chest. He gave her one gentle lick on the cheek—his final goodbye.

18
TIME EQUALS LOVE

Barb called the funeral home director, who already knew about Kristal's decision to die at home. Since it was 6:30 A.M. and Jeff would be up soon, I wanted them to hurry to pick up her body. I was afraid he'd wander sleepily out of his bedroom and be shocked to find his sister dead on the couch.

While waiting for the funeral team to arrive, I sat with Kristal on the couch, holding her, saying goodbye. It didn't feel spooky or uncomfortable to touch her, but it did bother me that her eyes refused to stay closed. After a few minutes of not blinking, they looked dry and painful, so I kept gently shutting them. But within a minute or two, her eyes would sneak back open, as if she didn't want to miss anything.

When the hearse arrived, Barb herded me into the kitchen. She wouldn't let me watch them pick her up because "you might not like the way the morticians handle her body."

Dad joined me in the kitchen. He did something so typical of him that I still picture him that way. He backed up against the kitchen counter, carefully planted his feet shoulder width apart on the linoleum, and motioned me into his arms. I folded, sobbing into his chest. His solid stance told me that he was prepared to stand there and hold me for as long as I needed to be held. In that moment, he was just like God to me.

Even with the pain of losing Mom so suddenly just a few weeks before, he was there to comfort me. Just like God,

He wasn't in a hurry, wasn't disgusted that I was weak enough to cry. He didn't bother to tell me it would be okay, didn't feel compelled to say anything at all. Instead, He cared enough to share my pain. I don't know how long I cried. Supported and upheld in the strong arms of both my Heavenly Father and the earthly one who so closely represented Him, I felt safe and protected.

And when I finally opened my eyes, I noticed the calendar on the kitchen wall. My heart stopped.

"Dad," I said with my mouth hanging open again. "Today is June 6."

"Huh?"

"Things have been so hectic that I forgot all about it. June 6 was the day Kristal chose as her wedding day."

"What wedding day?"

"I may not have told you this," I said. "The day doctors told us Kristal wasn't going to make it, we decided to plan her wedding. She chose June 6 as her wedding day."

"It's like she knew," I said, thinking out loud. "Like she really did marry Jesus. Like she knew she'd go to Him today. She's the bride of Christ, just like in the Bible. Wow!"

I didn't even hear Barb put Kristal's bedding in the washing machine and pick up her things in the living room. As if she was proud of her, Barb told me that Kristal hadn't even wet her pants or messed herself. I remember thinking it was weird that that information was significant enough to share. Yuck. But then I'd always known my daughter was extraordinary.

Within an hour, my sisters and brother arrived with quiet hugs and sad faces. Dad must have called them. Perhaps because it was still early on a Saturday morning, it seemed appropriate to tiptoe. We didn't want to wake Jeff. And it seemed more respectful.

Someone made coffee. They held each other, cried, and

whispered at the kitchen table. We all moved in slow motion, as if the world was in danger of stopping.

What was the appropriate thing to do now? We sat scattered around the house, not speaking, not feeling, just sort of numb, not knowing what to do next. If Miss Manners ever wrote instructions on how to handle the minutes and hours after a death, none of us had read them.

I didn't even try to control the tears. It wasn't an angry avalanche of tears, just a slow, lazy leak that started and stopped intermittently every time I realized, again, that Kristal was gone. It was like the grief kept pushing the air out of my lungs.

There was peace and stillness in the living room. The room felt empty even with all of us in it. Kristal's pain had gone, but our discomfort remained. The black cloud had dissipated, but the sun wasn't out. Surprisingly, it wasn't awful. Just empty.

I'd heard that God gives us a peace that passes all understanding. That's just what it was like. My mind told me I should be wailing, angry and cold, yet I felt peace. Sad, but peaceful too. It made no sense.

Rubbing his eyes, Jeff finally stumbled out of his bedroom and into my lap. He didn't seem surprised to find the whole family sitting on the couch where his sister should have been. When I told him Kristal was gone, he cried softly in my arms, but not nearly as long as I expected.

Jeff was scheduled to go to his dad's that day. Since choosing caskets was not something he needed to be involved in, I said goodbye to another of my children that day. At least I knew I'd see this one tomorrow.

I recognized the sound of Gary's VW van as he pulled down the driveway. "The bus" had had several different engines and been various shades of blue, green and peeling since I first saw it nearly two decades years earlier, but it looked better than ever as an antique. My family disappeared into some other room before I opened the door for him.

Even though we had been divorced for a dozen years, his hug felt vaguely familiar. Solid. Comfortable. But strange, like something from a past life. Words weren't necessary.

We sat alone in the living room, the enormity of our daughter's death a common bond of pain. It was quiet enough that I heard the air as it left his lungs. Even though he had visited a few days earlier, he clearly wasn't prepared. I told him about Kristal's last moments. About the peace on her face. That she no longer hurt.

The finality of it seemed to have surprised him. His head and shoulders drooped as he sat silently on the couch and his eyes stayed focused on the floor.

"I had it all planned, you know. She was going to live with me when she went to college. Then she'd get married and live right down the street. She'd have kids. I'd be the best grandpa ever. We were gonna be so close."

His voice cracked. He paused and swallowed hard a couple of times. Elbows on his knees, he pressed his fingers against his temples, then ran them slowly through his thick, dishwater blond hair.

Still not looking up, he said quietly, "Now none of that will ever happen. I had it all planned."

"Gary, how many guys out there think that?" I challenged him, "Don't tell ME that. Tell someone—but tell someone that doesn't know, someone who would benefit by that information. Tell all those guys out there who think nothing like this could ever happen to them. Write to Dear Abby. Join a divorced parents' group—tell someone who needs to know."

Emptiness filled the room as we sat facing each other on the cushions where Kristal had died only hours before. We laughed about the time she threw up in Grandma's purse on the windy road toward her house. We remembered the photo of Kristal in sunglasses and Grandpa Geno's extra-large

Budweiser t-shirt. We talked about her fetish for beef jerky and for dressing up as a bride.

"It's easier for you than it is for me," he finally said. "You have your faith."

"I suppose that's true," I said, thinking. "At least I know that she doesn't hurt anymore and that she'll never hurt again. Better than anything, I know I'll see her again. But you could have faith too, Gary. Got ten minutes? All you need to do is ask."

He waved me off, and I didn't push. We were strangely comfortable together. We sat there for an hour or so, allowing ourselves to feel our individual pain—I because I had lost my best friend, he because it was too late to know his daughter. My heart broke for all the other divorced fathers out there.

My mind went to the times she waited for him to pick her up for a weekend at his house. As a little girl, she would have her teddy bears, PJs, and favorite things packed. Anxious and excited, she awaited his 10 o'clock arrival. She planted her nose firmly against the leaded glass window that filled most of our front door, waiting.

A few minutes before the designated hour, she began to ask what time it was. About every thirty seconds. At 10 o'clock she picked up the suitcase and leaned against the door with it. By 10:07, her arms gave out and she dejectedly put it down and went back to her nose-against-the-door stance.

The "what time is it?" questions were soon replaced with "Where could dad be?" The minutes dragged by for both of us. When minutes became hours, they must have felt like an eternity to her 5-year-old heart.

Back then, it took only minutes for me to be angry at Gary for putting me in the position to have to make excuses for him. I don't think I was convincing for very long. But when I did say something I shouldn't have about her father, she wouldn't hear it. Her hands immediately clapped against her ears, and she absolutely refused to listen.

She defended him vehemently even after hours of nose-pressing. Many times, I cried in the next room as I watched her little body slump further and further into her velour rocking chair as she stoically waited, pretending to watch TV.

Although he lived only an hour from us, sometimes weeks or even months would crawl by without a word from her dad. After weeks in the hospital when Gary hadn't called or visited, even True Grit cried and asked, "Why can't I make him love me?"

A mother can only explain so much.

I know Gary loved her and would never have intentionally caused her pain. It wasn't that he didn't care. He was just one of those guys who never figured out how to show his love. Maybe he didn't know how. I don't think he had any idea how much his absence hurt her.

Somehow, someday, I hope other fathers can learn from the pain he so obviously felt as he sat on the couch that day.

19
GRIEF AND JOY

The day after Kristal died, I couldn't see any reason to get out of bed. In fact, when I opened my eyes the next morning, I couldn't figure out why the sun was up. As if nothing had changed, birds sang in the trees outside my window. I was confused. "What in the hell are they singing about?" I asked out loud, flinging my pillow over my head.

Hadn't they heard? Didn't they understand? The world was different now. My child was gone. Not just for the day, not just for the weekend—she was gone from my sight, gone from my hearing, gone from my side. I felt like my heart would burst right out of my body.

I pulled Mr. Ed around me, tucked myself in tight. No matter how hard I tried, I couldn't stop the tears. Pain seemed to hit me like waves. It doubled me over, then spit me out onto the hard, lonely beach to wait until the next bout hit just 30 seconds later.

In the night I woke up several times with what seemed to be a weight on me—as if someone or something evil was sitting on my chest. I couldn't fill my lungs with air. It was like one of those scary dreams you have sometimes—when someone is chasing you and you just know he's going to kill you and you run and you run but when you try to scream, nothing comes out of your mouth. It was that sort of panic.

As I had done before in one of those scary dreams, I called on Jesus. I knew I had to say His name out loud. Once

I got it out, I was better. The person on my chest got up and left. Not that he didn't show up again, but at least I was able to breathe.

Anyway, I just didn't see a reason to get up. I could hear my dad in the kitchen. He had shushed Jeff several times so he wouldn't wake me and the two of them were making pancakes, Dad's specialty. But that only lasted so long. After an hour or so, dad tapped on the door.

"Shirl?" he whispered about 9 o'clock.

"What?" I grouched from under my covers.

"Do you want some breakfast? Want to get up?"

Jeff sneaked under Dad's arm and Dad couldn't grab him before he jumped onto the bed. He climbed under the covers and wrapped his little arms around my neck. No one's arms had ever felt so good. As if it was his job to comfort me, this sweet boy patted my head softly while another wave hit. I just clung to him and cried, grateful that he was still with me.

But a 6-year-old boy can only take so much cuddling. Soon he was out the door. Again Dad asked if I wanted to get up. I didn't. But eventually, people need bathrooms. As much as I wanted to, I couldn't stay there forever.

I was concerned about Jeff and kept trying to figure out how to help him through his sister's death. After a long talk, he finally admitted that he was upset.

"She just disappeared," he said, "You took her away, and I didn't even get to say goodbye."

I shook my head. I'd thought I was doing the right thing by taking her body away, but it's so hard to know what people need, even your own children.

"How about writing her a letter to say goodbye?" I suggested. "Then we'll take it to her and tuck it in with her."

We had talked about this. Kristal had said I could come and see her in her casket "if you have to." I had to and apparently, so did Jeff. Dad, Jeff and I went to the funeral home.

Nothing can prepare you to see your child in a coffin. It took my breath away. Made my eyes leak and my knees weak. She was laying there in her peach silk prom dress, surrounded by what looked like pillows of soft pink fabric, looking more peaceful and beautiful than I had expected.

Without much ado, Jeff slipped his color crayoned letter into her hand. "Thanks for being a good big sister," it said. "I'll miss you. Love, Jeff."

My fashion sense kicked in and I noticed that she wasn't wearing earrings. We couldn't have that! I took off my favorite pearl earrings and proceeded to put them into the ears we'd had pierced so long ago. I practically had to crawl in there with her to get the one on the far side to go in, but it finally worked. I almost expected her to rise up and yell, "Get off me!" but she didn't say a word. Now she looked ready to meet her Bridegroom, I thought.

Dad took some photos, then we left. I knew I wouldn't be able to look at them right away, but in case I was ever ready, I wanted to know they existed.

The day of the memorial service was sunny, bright and clear. Kristal had requested that we bury her privately so that no one had to "look at me in the coffin while you talk about me."

So, about a dozen family members and a couple of close friends gathered around a casket-sized hole in the ground in the freshly mowed and watered Fox Island Cemetery. Pastor Andy began speaking. Dad caught my eye and nodded toward the hearse, which was about 20 feet away. Through the open doors I saw the coffin. A small chuckle escaped me. Dad and I discussed the matter with our eyes for a minute, then I spoke up.

"Hey, Andy," I said, interrupting a perfectly lovely and

moving speech. "I think we should get Kristal involved in all of this."

"Oh, oh. Of course," he sputtered.

I hadn't thought to assign pall bearers, so with a shrug, we all went to get her. When I picked up the front, right handle of the coffin and began to pull, someone, I don't remember who (but obviously someone who didn't know me well) mentioned the word inappropriate and tried to scoot me out of the way.

"Heck, I carried her for years," I said. "I'd like to do it one last time."

With the added weight, the heels of my white sandals stuck in the grass and I had to yank them out with every step. That done, we quickly finished up the short ceremony and headed off for the Memorial Service.

Hundreds of people poured onto the expansive lawn on the edge of the softball field where Kristal used to play. I was grateful that George, a retired friend from church had thought to organize parking attendants to direct traffic on this little Fox Island lane. Pots of bright flowers and a wooden podium with a cross on the front created a focus. It was a big field with a lot of flowers, I noted.

Our friend Bob, who taught at Kristal's high school and had put together the fundraiser for her earlier, had organized a group of about 10 of her friends to sing Michael Smith's *Friends*. Not one of them made it through the line "Friends are friends forever" without breaking down. They released multi-colored balloons, and we all watched them float off into the cloudless sky.

About a dozen of the doctors and nurses I had come to love showed up, making me wonder how many of their days off they spent at such events.

And when the service was over, friends lined up to shake my hand and dispense hugs and extend their sympathy. It was wonderful to see so many old friends, so at least in that sense, the day was as sweet as any wedding reception. I kept thinking that this was just as Kristal had pictured her wedding—outside in a big field with lots of flowers.

Strangely enough, the person who most fell apart at the memorial service was Jerry. He fell into my arms like he expected me to hold him up. Through the first honest-to-goodness tears I'd ever seen him shed, he mumbled into my shoulder. "Oh, it's just…God… and Kristal," he snuffled.

And I was not sympathetic. It was too late for him to start caring. Like most women, I remembered his every failing—the times he hadn't asked how she was doing, hadn't visited, hadn't been there to help with Jeff, hadn't whatever. I wasn't ready to forgive or comfort him. Too bad, because I've never again seen Jerry so open to the Lord as he was that day.

Inside, my Bible Study Fellowship friends bustled around a 20-foot table topped with white linen, candles and an enormous array of delectable salads, fruits, hot dishes and desserts. These precious ladies buzzed around polishing silver and fanning out napkins, making the room look exactly like a wedding reception. Kristal would have loved it.

But just as any mother of the bride, I went home without my daughter. God promises never to give us more than we can handle. This was close. Oh so close.

The next day I took a picnic blanket and a cassette player to the cemetery. I carefully laid the blanket on the grass beside Kristal's grave and played her the tape of the ceremony. I told her who came and who said what and about all she missed. And sitting there alone in the grass, I cried and cried.

That was the last time I ever felt Kristal's presence.

Monday, Jeff came home from school very unhappy. He and Mike had gotten into a fight with some bigger boys on the playground.

"They were teasing me," he admitted after some coaxing.

"About what? Do you know these boys? What were they teasing you about?"

"One said, 'We heard your sisss-ter died. What did she do, look at your face?'"

"Whattt?" I stammered, livid. I couldn't believe little kids could be so cruel! I grabbed my boy and held him tight.

"Another kid said, 'Did you kill her?'" he whispered into my neck.

"Auuggh! That's it! You don't have to go to school tomorrow. In fact, there's only a few more days of school anyway. You can take the rest of the year off. I'll talk to your teacher tomorrow."

I had to pry, but he told me a few more stories of the abuse he'd been taking at school. Turns out he and Mike had been putting up with this on a regular basis. My heart broke for the pain this six-year-old had been enduring because he happened to have a sister who was sick. I just didn't get it.

A few days after Kristal's funeral, Gary came over to pick up some of her things for his stepdaughters. We sat on the couch and talked for a few minutes.

"I want to help pay Kristal's medical bills," he said out of the clear blue sky.

I had to try hard to stay upright and not choke and fall over in a dead faint. In the nearly two years of Kristal's illness, he had never offered such a thing—even when I asked.

My insurance had paid roughly $800,000 worth of medical bills, which meant my 10% share amounted to about $80,000. I had been making payments for nearly two years now, but knew it would be a long time before my balance was anywhere near zero.

I showed Gary my enormous basketful of bills and

explained that each time she was admitted to the hospital Kristal had been assigned another account number. The bills were stacked nice and neat, in order of their appearance, but finance has never been an exact science for me. I didn't know where my balance stood. So we went to the phone, and I called the accounting department at the hospital to find out.

I explained that I wanted an exact balance so I could begin paying it off. The woman on the end of the phone punched in Kristal's social security number.

"There are 38 accounts to reconcile," she said, clicking her tongue. "I estimate that the balance will be around $40, maybe $41,000, but this will take some time. I'll add it all up and get back you by Wednesday."

I gave her my work number and hung up. I hoped that Gary would write a check then and there, but he left with his checkbook firmly fitted in the pocket of his fashionably faded tight Levis. He still looked good in them, I must say.

Wednesday came and went. Thursday, Friday passed and I never heard from the accounting lady. With each passing day, she moved further down my list of reliability. People who make promises they don't keep generally don't last long on my list.

By the following Monday afternoon, this woman was in the same category as my ex-husbands. When she finally did call me at work I was busy, and plenty skeptical. I left Neen with the customers out front and went to my office to take the call. I stood at my desk and grabbed a pen to write down the number she was about to give me—the amount it would take me another couple of years to pay off, even with Gary's help.

"Oh, is it Wednesday already?" I asked, sarcastic right off the bat.

"I'm sorry, I called to tell you that I don't have a balance," she began.

"Then why are you calling?"

"Well, I've been working very hard on this."

Then why don't you have a balance, you idiot?
I thought. *All you had to do was add up a column of 38
figures. And you work in the accounting department, for
heaven's sake!*

"When WILL you have a balance?" I asked, drawing
big, dark circles on a pile of papers.

"Well, my boss and I are working together..." I didn't
hear the rest. *Morons,* I thought. *Even the two of you can't
add???!! You must have a big old calculator!*

"We won't be sending bills to your home any more,"
she said, sounding as if she thought she was making perfect
sense.

"What do you MEAN you won't send bills home?
Where in the world ARE you going to send them?"

"You don't understand," she said.

Duh, I thought. My circles had dug holes through
several layers of paper at this point.

"No, I don't understand! Explain it to me, will you?" I
said, shaking my head in frustration.

"Well, the state will pick up some of the blood
transfusion costs and my boss and I are working on the rest.
There is no balance."

"What do you MEAN there is no balance?" I asked,
exasperated. "How can there be no balance?"

"I'm trying to tell you that the balance is zero. You
don't owe us anything."

"How can that BE?" I said, stunned.

"Well," she said, still patient in spite of my irritation,
"sometimes people donate money to Mary Bridge. Their wills
state that they want to help pay off the bills of people who
lose children. The money is coming from people like that."

What? Was it possible? Tears began to fall. Soon they
were splashing on my scribbled, ripped papers. I sank to my

knees in front of my desk.

"How can that be?" I said, much more softly this time. "Do you mean that I don't have to pay? Who can I thank for this?"

"Oh, a whole bunch of people. You don't know any of them."

Through humble tears, I profusely thanked this marvelous woman, who only moments ago had been an idiot in my mind. Then, still on my knees, I sobbed. There was no one to thank...

But before I even completed that thought, I knew exactly who to thank. God. My incredibly wonderful and gracious and generous and faithful God. My God who was more faithful to me than any husband I've ever heard of. The one I could count on to take care of me in the most dire circumstances.

The one thing I regret is that Gary never had to pay a dime. But I did love calling to tell him about this latest miracle. I pray that one day he too will find faith in my incredible, extravagant, tender-hearted and ultra-reliable God.

Following Kristal's death, I had a lot of what I called grief attacks. They affected me in all sorts of ways, but mostly my brain felt as pink and melty as cotton candy. The simplest decisions just wouldn't be made. I sometimes found myself standing at the kitchen counter with a can of corn in one hand and a can of green beans in the other. Five minutes later I still had not decided which to serve with dinner.

Especially at first, I resented people who were having a good time. If I caught a glimpse of someone laughing on a street corner, a flash of anger appeared out of nowhere. *"Have you no shame? How could you laugh at a time like this?"* Laughing felt disloyal to Kristal and for weeks was unthinkable to me.

I was offended at people's insensitivity. My good friend

Mark didn't even attend Kristal's memorial service. "Those things are hard for me," he later explained.

"Yeah, well, burying my daughter was a piece of cake for me," I felt like answering. "Thanks for all your support." I could have smacked his head.

Some found it easier not to mention this enormous event—as if they could avoid tromping through three feet of water by daintily holding the hems of their pants out of the way. I'm sure their intent was good. They just didn't want to make me cry—and let's face it—I did spend a couple of hours of each day in tears at that point.

I did try to work. For at least part of every day I went in to the store while Dad and Jeff went fishing or to the beach. It didn't seem to matter if I was there or not. Business was very slow.

One woman left me a note at work that said, "I was so glad you weren't here when I came in today. I just didn't know what to say to you." Some were clearly afraid my misfortune was something they could catch. Some would go on and on about their uncle's funeral or some poor sod who had previously been in my shoes.

Worse than those who avoided me were the ones who tried to explain it. "It's God's will," or "Everything works together for those who love God and are called according to His purposes." I wanted to shout, "Too bad He didn't want YOUR child for His purposes!"

The most helpful people were just there. They didn't offer explanations or excuses; sometimes they didn't say anything at all. They may have said they were sorry or just sat with me in silence. They cried with me. They offered hugs. The most helpful people asked how I was and listened if I felt like talking, but didn't pressure me and didn't feel the need to give me all the answers. I believed only God really knew the reasons behind it all.

The why of Kristal's death still baffled me. Then

I remembered *Angel Unaware,* a book that had greatly impacted me when I was about 12. I found another copy and reread it. Dale Evans Rogers wrote it from the viewpoint of her two-year-old daughter, Robin, who was born with multiple health problems including Down Syndrome. In the book, Robin sits on God's lap and tells him all she has accomplished on Earth in her short two years there. It's a sweet, touching book that made me cry all the way through it—again—but it gave me such hope.

I searched the Bible to see if Dale was right. Turns out there is no guarantee that we all get to live a full 65 or 87 or 104 years. All it says on the subject is that God has things all planned. He knows how many hairs are on our heads and how many days we each are assigned on Earth. He knows. He doesn't tell us, but He knows.

One thing I'm absolutely certain of is that I'll see Kristal again. The Bible says we will meet our loved ones in the sky, that we will come from the west and they from the east. I hang onto that thought and often imagine what it will be like to meet in the clouds. Cool, I'm sure. Very cool.

But I wondered. Would I have wanted to know that Kristal only had 16 years? Would I have protected her unmercifully? Coddled and spoiled her and created a monster? Probably. I loved being Kristal's mom, (well, most days). But I decided that God was kind and wise not to tell me that I would only have 16 years with her.

I thought of the other children I knew who had died—Clayton, a five-year-old named Erik, some in the hospital and some children of friends. Each of them seemed to have lived in high gear, almost as if they knew they had to squeeze every ounce of living out of their days. There was an enormous hole in my life since Kristal was gone, but God was helping me make peace with it.

Jeff was having a hard time too. He was alternately

whiny, withdrawn and obnoxious. One day I actually caught him kicking the dog! I didn't know how to handle it. I had tried giving him a break and letting him be. I tried cracking down and punishing him. Nothing seemed to be working. So, I tried the logical thing—talking to him. I remember sitting in a chair while he stood beside me.

"What am I going to do with you, Jeff?" I asked with my arm around his waist. "I know you're hurting so I've tried to be understanding. I've tried reasoning with you. I don't know what else to do. How can I help you?"

This six-year-old didn't say a word. Instead, he took my hand in his and smacked his own bottom with it. I was stunned.

"Are you saying that you can't control yourself right now? That I need to do that for you?" I stammered.

He nodded.

"Oh, Jeff, I'm so sorry. I've been so wrapped up in my own pain that I haven't helped you at all, have I?

"I know you're angry. I'm angry too. Tell you what. Maybe you need something to smack when you get mad. The dog is off limits, but let's go find a pillow you can hit. Whenever you feel like hitting something, go get your pillow and punch it as much as you need to. If all the stuffing comes out, we'll buy you a new pillow. Deal?"

"Deal," he said, already headed for the bedroom.

I held the pillow up like it was a person. At first, he thought it was silly, and I had to talk him into really punching the thing. But soon he smacked it over and over, growling as he did. And when he was done, he stood back with a smile on his face. Over the next several weeks, I had to send him to find his pillow regularly. He never did wear out the first one, but the pillow seemed to help.

But one thing I desperately needed to know was that Kristal was okay. I longed to see her just as I envisioned her:

in glorious white robes, preferably standing beside Jesus. It didn't seem like too much to ask. I told God all about it, but didn't see a thing. No visions, no impressions. Not even an imaginative cloud formation or a suggestive reflection in a puddle. Nothing.

It had been only ten weeks since Mom died. After Kristal's funeral we needed to get away. Dad suggested taking his motor home on a tour of the northwest corner of Washington State. It felt so good to think about something else for a change.

We hiked through the Olympic Peninsula's beautiful old-growth forest, winding our way around 600-year-old fir trees. A ranger told us that the trunks of one of these giants was 14-feet in diameter. He lined the whole tour group up to try to hold hands around it to prove his point, but the thing was too big around and we couldn't touch.

Over the last months I'd learned how much God loved me. He had showed me on a daily basis. But with my arms wrapped around one of those mammoth trees, I realized I was not the only thing that mattered to God. It was hard to feel like the center of the world beside their enormity. He had other things to take care of, too. Other people He loved. Others whose lives He was orchestrating at that very moment. He was responsible for every tree and animal I had seen that day—and all the others I hadn't seen, for heaven's sake. God, I realized, is a very busy guy!

That night we camped on the Washington coast. This was no surfing beach. Basically it was an enormous gray terrain, the length of five football fields laid end to end, strewn with driftwood and the remains of people's old campfires. Irregular, overlapping lines of dried white foam looked like old lace that some deranged old decorator had dragged behind her on the fine gray sand.

Jeff and I walked down from our campsite for a closer look. There were a few sweat-shirted people braving the wind to search for shells or rocks, but there was mostly a wide open expanse of sand, surf, and sky.

Jeff drew circles in the sand with pieces of driftwood that seemed way too big for him to drag around. Then, with the mind of a six-year-old architect, he began building a fort. I sat on a log. The wind whipped my hair around my face, hiding my tears. I watched for what seemed like hours as perfectly timed waves broke and crashed and flowed up onto the sand.

As the sun slid under the horizon, I realized that if I sat there forever, I would never see the last of them. Only our Creator saw the first wave, and they'll keep rolling in, one after another after another, long after I'm gone.

"I am faithful," God seemed to be saying. "Faithful enough to send these waves in, one after the other, ever since the beginning of the world."

My life, I thought as I sat there, *is a long way from perfect. But a lot of things that make it that way are my choices, not God's.*

Now God seemed to be teaching me, healing me, through the wonders of nature. Those waves and trees revealed His patience and faithfulness. I felt as though I'd caught a glimmer of eternity through His eyes. I came to understand that the same God who tends giant trees for 600 years watches over me. The One who controls the waves, the entire universe, is in charge of my life.

I had asked for a glimpse of my daughter. I realized as I sat on that log that God had given me something far better—a long renewing look at His character. Something to go on with, rather than something to look back on. His love is as constant as the waves rolling in on that shore.

I thanked Him then for faithfully hanging onto me—through the divorce and the aloneness, through the heavy load of single parenthood, through the long years in the hospital, through Kristal's death, through it all. He had never loosened His grip. There were days when I came close to struggling out of His grasp, but I knew it was me, not Him, that wanted to pull away. Through it all, He held me close.

Unlike either of my husbands, God had proven that He wouldn't run, wouldn't leave, wouldn't quit. He'd be there, no matter how tough things got. I knew I could count on Him like no mortal man.

20

SHE
CRIED FOR US

As Kristal's 17th birthday approached, I had an increasingly hard time. What could I do? I wanted to bake a cake, plan a party, something like I'd done for every other birthday of her life. Grandma Hennie called with an idea.

Even after Gary and I divorced, this precious lady refused to let me out of the family. She continued to be part of my life, calling and visiting whenever she could. And she and Kristal always had secrets. Henrietta told me about her last conversation with Kristal.

"Kristal asked me to be your mom," Henrietta said matter-of-factly.

"What?" I was stunned.

"Your mom had just died. She knew she was dying and didn't want you to be alone. She thought you'd need someone to watch out for you after she was gone, so she asked me to be your mom. Made me promise. She didn't want you to be alone."

I melted. How much did God love me to give me 16 years with this sensitive, thoughtful child? With all of the miserable things she faced on a daily basis, how could Kristal have been thinking of me and how I would handle her death?

"Let's go pick out a memorial stone for Kristal's grave," Grandma Hennie suggested.

"Just what every 17-year-old wants for her birthday—a

gravestone. But it is about the only thing she really needs. Okay."

I prayed and thought long and hard about what to engrave on the headstone. After all, this would be written in stone for all the world to see. One friend had "Dragons live forever, not so little boys" engraved on his son's. His 8-year-old had died of a brain tumor when Puff the Magic Dragon was popular. But I needed something that spoke of hope, of what I believe.

So, I had engraved in stone:

Kristal Lynn Nieland
August 14, 1970-June 6, 1987
Ours for 16 years, Thine for eternity

On her birthday I baked her a cake anyway—chocolate peanut butter, of course—and had my own little celebration. It wasn't much of a party, but I drove to the cemetery, sat down on a blanket and cut the cake. I took a couple of flats of red geraniums and planted them to form an eight-foot cross on top of her grave. It was so big that pilots flying over Fox Island could see it from their planes. I even sang Happy Birthday to her. I think I cried through the entire party. It was beautiful and heartbreaking at the same time.

Other things surprised me about having a child in the ground. Whenever the temperatures dropped, I kept worrying that Kristal would be cold under there. Ridiculous, I know, but I kept wondering what kind of mother I was not to have put a sweater or wrap on her. And what kind of wrap goes with a prom dress anyway? I think that's why proms are always as close as they can get to summer—so no one has to figure it out.

I also kept thinking that she was away. Maybe at camp or visiting a friend for the weekend. That she'd be back any time. I scanned crowds, sure that I'd see her headed my way.

When something funny happened, I'd sometimes turn like I just had to tell her, only to be a little surprised that she wasn't there. Yes, I knew she was gone, but it was like I kept forgetting that part. She'd been beside me for almost 17 years so not having her there took some getting used to.

Over those awful, empty months that followed, the teardrop Kristal had shed as she took her last breath drove me crazy. It was obviously misplaced. I couldn't get it out of my mind. I asked the Lord over and over again to show me what that teardrop meant—why she had cried.

About three o'clock one morning, I felt an urge to get up and grab a pencil. Loving thoughts began dropping into my mind, as if God Himself sat beside me at the kitchen table. I started to write down His explanation of that teardrop.

Typical of her gutsy character, He said, she didn't cry for herself in that one lonely teardrop, but for those she was leaving behind.

She cried for me, He said tenderly, for the wedding I would never see, the grandchildren I would never hold, for the awful empty places that would remain permanently inside of me.

She cried for Jeff, for the love of his big sister who wasn't there anymore, that she didn't give him any final advice on how to live his life to her standards.

She cried for the shock of her teenage friends, for the new way they would have to look at life, knowing now, as teenagers often don't, that it does have an end.

She cried for her father, for the guilt she knew he would feel, for the times together they missed when she was young and now would never have.

She cried for my extended family, that they would have to endure another loss, another funeral, another empty chair at the Christmas dinner table. We hadn't even begun to get accustomed to her grandmother's death and now we had hers to bear.

As I sat in the kitchen that night, it finally sank in. That tear was not for herself. She was not the type to feel sorry for herself, to cry for her own pain, for what she had endured because of her illness, for what she might miss here on earth, or for the dreams she would never satisfy. She cried only for us, those who would always feel the pain of her death.

I hadn't realized until several hours after she breathed her last breath and shed that solitary tear, that the date was June 6.

She went to be with her bridegroom, Jesus, on the exact day she had chosen as her wedding day. I only wish I could have sung the Dum, Dum, Da Dum and watched her step-toe-step down the aisle. Wish I could have seen Him looking at her with what must be incredible blue eyes.

She had joined Jesus, and though I could no longer see her, I knew she would never cry again.

Kristal's Wedding

DEDICATION AND APPRECIATION TO...

- Kristal, my amazingly brave and charming daughter who was really just a normal kid.
- Bob and Jeani Leslie, Sharon Molin, plus Andy and Margie Snodgrass and the saints at Fox Island Alliance Church who helped me find Jesus.
- The incredible people of Fox Island and Gig Harbor, who cared, prayed, and gave to help God answer our prayers.
- Dr. Dan Niebrugge, Joan Cooley, and the other staff at Mary Bridge Children's Hospital for their care, kindness and expertise.
- Jon Ballard and the anonymous donors who generously paid off bills that were not theirs to pay.
- Scott and Sandi Tompkins, who've spent years reading, editing, teaching, and mentoring me.
- Audra Baumgarth, Dorothy Spero, and the other talented members of Sandi's Kona Writer's Group.
- Laurel Cleary and the team who believes in me, supports and encourages me. I couldn't have done this without you.
- Susan Westbrook, Sam Hubbard and Bob Brown for the website, the cover and the photos.
- My son Jeff, who finally said, "Quit thinking publishing and start thinking ministry." May this book minister to hearts all over the world.
- The biggest thanks goes to my Lord and Savior. He gets all of the credit. He sat beside me as I wrote and provided me with incredible friends who helped me get this into print. Oh, and He knows my faults and loves me anyway.

You all rock!

Made in the USA